IS THE

BIBLE

TRUE . . . REALLY?

[A DIALOGUE ON SKEPTICISM, EVIDENCE, AND TRUTH]

COFFEE HOUSE

CHRONICLES

IS THE

BIBLE

TRUE . . . REALLY?

JOSH MCDOWELL
AND DAVE STERRETT

MOODY PUBLISHERS
CHICAGO

All Scripture quotations, unless otherwise indicated, are taken from the *Holy Bible, New International Version*®, NIV®. Copyright ©1973, 1978, 1984 by Biblica, Inc.™ Used by permission of Zondervan. All rights reserved worldwide.

All Scripture quotations marked NASB are taken from the *New American Standard Bible*®, Copyright © 1960, 1962, 1963, 1968, 1971, 1972, 1973, 1975, 1977, 1995 by The Lockman Foundation. Used by permission. (www.Lockman.org)

All Scripture quotations marked NLT are taken from the *Holy Bible, New Living Translation*, copyright © 1996, 2004. Used by permission of Tyndale House Publishers, Inc., Wheaton, Illinois 60189, U.S.A. All rights reserved.

All Scripture quotations marked ESV are taken from *The Holy Bible, English Standard Version*. Copyright © 2000, 2001 by Crossway Bibles, a division of Good News Publishers. Used by permission. All rights reserved.

All Scripture quotations marked KJV are taken from the King James Version.

Edited by Paul Santhouse
Interior design: Ragont Design
Sterrett Photo: Katherine Robertson

Cover design: Faceout Studio
Cover image: iStock #000001950627
McDowell Photo: Barbara Gannon

Library of Congress Cataloging-in-Publication Data

McDowell, Josh.
    Is the Bible true-- really? : a dialogue on skepticism, evidence, and truth / Josh McDowell and Dave Sterrett.
        p. cm. -- (The coffeehouse chronicles ; 1)
    Includes bibliographical references.
    ISBN 978-0-8024-8766-7
    1. Bible—Evidences, authority, etc. I. Sterrett, Dave. II. Title.
    BS480.M383 2011
    220.1—dc22

                                            2010039594

We hope you enjoy this book from Moody Publishers. Our goal is to provide high-quality, thought-provoking books and products that connect truth to your real needs and challenges. For more information on other books and products written and produced from a biblical perspective, go to www.moodypublishers.com or write to:

Moody Publishers
820 N. LaSalle Boulevard
Chicago, IL 60610

1 3 5 7 9 10 8 6 4 2

Printed in the United States of America

To

Dr. Robert Saucy,
my professor and mentor for three years.
Who always challenged me to love Jesus,
study the Scriptures, and pursue Truth.
—Josh

To

Dr. Norman L. Geisler
and Dr. Daniel B. Wallace
—Dave

CONTENTS

One

INTELLECTUAL SKEPTICISM

Mid-September

"HOW MANY of you all—or should I say *y'all*—grew up in Texas?"

About half of the hands in the classroom went up.

"Good, glad to see it. My wife and I have enjoyed living here for almost twelve years now. We've learned a few things too. For example, here in the South, especially right here in Dallas, the *buckle* of the Bible Belt, we dare not question the historical authority of the books of the Bible, or we're damned to hell!"

A few chuckles echoed across the small auditorium. Dr. William Peterson,

Distinguished Professor of Religious Studies and a renowned expert on ancient textual criticism, was well known for his views. Smiling wryly, he continued, "Honestly, I appreciate the concern these fundamentalists, Catholics, and evangelicals have for our souls, and I believe they are genuinely sincere—just sincerely misled."

Nick, a freshman at Opal University, listened intently as Dr. Peterson went on. "Conservative Christians are quick to judge those of us in academia for our views, but my question for them would be, 'What is the historical basis for believing the Bible really is the inerrant Word of God?' I want to know what persuades them to actually believe that the copies of the Bible translated today are even close to what was originally written down? It *sounds* good and faithful, but what are the facts? That's what we're here to explore. Are you ready for the facts?"

The room fell silent as the professor paused for effect. "Here are the facts that leading scholars all across the country agree upon. *We don't even have the words that these fundamentalist Christians tell us God inerrantly inspired.* That's right. All we have are words copied by scribes—sometimes correctly but certainly not always. We have error-ridden copies that are centuries removed from the originals and different from them in thousands of ways."[1]

Nick's heart raced as he listened to the professor contradict what his pastor back home at Park Springs Community Church had taught the congregation. He sensed in his spirit this was his time to be bold for Christ and take a stand for the Lord. "That's not true!" he declared. "How dare you question God's Word."

The professor, somewhat taken aback by the student's interruption, responded kindly. "Very well, why don't you tell us what *is* true. What's not accurate about what I just said?"

Nick, now feeling a tad embarrassed and put on the spot, raised his voice. "Well, I'm a Christian and I believe the Bible is the inspired Word of God. I accept it as the Word of God by *faith*! Hebrews says, 'Without faith it is impossible to please God,' and since God is sovereign and we are just human beings, who are we to question His sovereignty? Also, the Bible says, 'All Scripture is God-breathed and is useful for teaching, rebuking, correcting and training in righteousness so that everyone will always be prepared to give an answer.'"

Dr. Peterson smiled and nodded. "I admire your personal faith and concern to quote portions of Hebrews 11 and 2 Timothy 3. Would you remind me of your name?"

"I'm Nick."

"I'm glad you're in this class, Nick. I remember memorizing those same verses myself. Looking back, I think it was when I attended Calvin Christian Academy during my early teens." Noting Nick's look of surprise, he continued,

"By the way, Nick, I think 2 Timothy 3 ends by saying, 'so that the man of God may be thoroughly equipped for every good work.' Perhaps, you were conflating it with 1 Peter 3:15, which mentions giving an answer or defense. That's okay, and really beside the point. What I was saying earlier, Nick, is that we really can't be sure the original book of Hebrews and the letter of 2 Timothy actually *said* the words you just quoted and that we both memorized. We don't have the 'original' of the Bible. The Bibles that you and I own have been radically changed over the past two thousand years."

"I don't believe that!" Nick blurted out.

"Oh? Would you care to educate us then?" asked the distinguished professor. The rest of the class murmured their annoyance at this rude, outspoken Christian.

"Well . . . um," Nick stumbled. "You can't, uh, I mean it's not only about the words, Professor. God continues to change lives. I experience the presence of Jesus in my life every day. And . . . um . . . oh yeah, I remember—when I went to youth camp in Tyler we had this former atheist speak to us and he told us his testimony and shared that we have archeological evidence and old historical manuscripts, or copies of the Bible, that verify God's Word. Professor, this former atheist is now a Christian!" Nick asserted this last part with confidence, believing the Holy Spirit had helped him finish stronger than he started.

"Nick, it certainly is true that we have manuscripts or copies of the early letters and gospels written, but what *type* of manuscripts is the question! I've looked at some of these manuscripts myself, Nick, and the number of variants, or differences, between various handwritten copies is in the hundreds of thousands!"[2] The majority of scholars in the country have come to recognize these facts. For example, a man I respect, Bart Ehrman, the head of the religion department at the University of North Carolina, Chapel Hill, has published some excellent academic works on textual criticism."

Dr. Peterson took a few steps closer to his students and sat on his stool near the front row where Nick was sitting. "Nick, I admire your sincere faith and I respect your religion, but the purpose of this class is to study religion *historically*. Class, let me ask you a question. Where is the *original* Bible that God inspired? Is it located in some museum? Does anyone know? Nick? Anybody?"

The class was silent, and by this time Nick was speechless as well.

"Come on, class, join the conversation. Anyone can speak up and help Nick out!" After a few awkward moments, the professor continued, "It's okay, Nick. Nobody knows. Listen to me, class. *We don't have the original.* There is no evidence that a 'God' inspired these letters. If this God of the Bible existed and was all-powerful, don't you think He would have cleared up the confusion for us all? For example, if you grew up going to church like I did, or like our friend Nick, your Bible probably has four gospels in the New Testament. But did you know there were many other gospels that were *not* included? What about the *Gospel of Thomas*, or the gospels of Philip or Mary Magdalene?[3]

"Students, I care about your personal beliefs. But I also care about your intellectual honesty in all areas—including the history of religion. I wish I had time to explain all of this to you today, but we'll get to it as the semester progresses. The message of Christianity is nothing new or unique. When I began studying biblical literature in graduate school, I discovered that stories of dying and rising gods, virgin births, and miracle workers were already widespread throughout the known world when the gospels were written.[4] We'll look into these things in more depth the next time we're together. Class dismissed."

Two

THE CARUTH HAVEN COFFEEHOUSE

NICK STORMED OUT of class furious and frustrated. As he walked by the science hall he heard a familiar voice. "Nick! Nick! How are you?"

He turned and saw Andrea, a biology major he had met the first day of orientation, cutting across the lawn to catch up with him.

"Hey, Andrea," Nick said.

"Nick, are you okay? You seem really upset."

"I'm all right, Andrea. It's just that my religion professor, Dr. Peterson, said some things I don't agree with."

"You have Dr. Peterson? I loved his

class when I had him last year! What did he say?"

"It's hard to explain. He and I just don't see eye to eye on some things. Man, he's got some strange ideas!"

Andrea smiled. "Nick, that's what you told me the first time we got into a spiritual conversation, remember? I'm sure it will be okay. We're still friends, right? Look, I'm headed over to the Caruth Haven Coffeehouse to study for a few hours. Why don't you come with me so we can talk about it?"

Nick looked at his watch, and then nodded. "All right. I've got some time before my next class."

Later, at a table by the window, Andrea took a sip of her caramel macchiato and looked at Nick. "So, what's on your mind, Nick? What did Dr. Peterson say?"

"Andrea, you know I have a personal relationship with Jesus, right? I believe Scripture is God-breathed and Jesus is the way, the truth, and the life. But Dr. Peterson told us the Bible has been changed, and that the Bibles we have today aren't even true!"

"Nick, I understand that this is hard for you, but I took his class and I'm pretty sure that Dr. Peterson is right."

"Here we go again," said Nick, sighing.

"Nick, the Bible *has* been changed, but I still think it's an inspiring book like the works of Homer, Virgil, and Plato. I understand what you're going through, though. It was hard for me to accept until I started reading other religious books outside of my own circle. When I attended St. Mary's Academy in high school, *not one* of my theology instructors told me how the Catholic Church chose what books to put in the Bible. They also didn't tell me the copies of the Bibles used today by both Catholics and Protestants have been drastically transformed throughout history, sometimes intentionally by religious leaders. It makes sense though since they've been copied over and over for more than two thousand years."

Nick stared out the window, chewing on his stir stick.

"There's another thing, too," continued Andrea. "My church never once told me that the Christian story plagiarized and borrowed from pagan myths that were around long before Christianity!"

"Hey, Dr. Peterson said something about that too! What's that all about, anyway? Is that what Dan Brown was talking about in his novels?"

"Nick, it's history. Dr. Peterson told us numerous other stories: Mythras, Appolonius, Sabbati, and others. Have you seen that YouTube video called *Zeitgeist, The Greatest Story Ever Sold*?"

"The what?"

"Okay, check this out."

Andrea turned her MacBook around so Nick could watch the clip. He plugged his headphones in, hit play, and heard about religious leaders throughout history who had similar life characteristics to Jesus. The video implied that Christianity simply plagiarized from other religious stories that were circulating years before Jesus' birth. Names like Attis of Greece, Krishna of India, Dionysus of Greece, and Mithra of Persia were included in the video. The narrator described how, based on astrology, each of these religious leaders was born of a virgin on December 25, discovered by a star in the East, was adored by three kings, began teaching at twelve, was baptized into ministry at thirty, had twelve disciples, performed miracles, was known as the "Lamb of God" and "The Light," and was crucified, buried, and resurrected on the third day.

Nick was speechless during the entire video except for the one time he rolled his eyes and said, "Noooo waaaayyyy."

At the end of the clip, Nick looked at Andrea. "Hey, regardless of what Dr. Peterson and that stupid YouTube video say, I still believe that the Bible is God's Word, by *faith*!"

Nick didn't want to admit it to Andrea, but for a few seconds he had questioned the truthfulness of his Christian beliefs.

"Andrea," Nick continued. "God's Word is not going to come back void and I trust that His Spirit speaks through me when I don't know what to say. Even when I don't have all the answers, God is sovereign and is changing lives through His Spirit. Besides, that video is probably just a hoax. I'm out of here, Andrea. I need to get to class."

Andrea watched him fill his backpack.

Before leaving the table, Nick asked, "Hey, are you going to that party on Friday?"

"What party?"

"The one at Jessica's," responded Nick.

"Yes! I'm there, but what about you? I didn't think you were the drinking type."

"I'm not. But you know, God has called me to be salt and light. Even Jesus came eating and drinking with sinners like you, Andrea! Just kidding, but Jesus did say, 'It's not the healthy who need a doctor but the sick.'"

"Nick, you're goofy, but I like you. You may hold some old-school views of the Bible, but at least you're genuine."

As the weeks passed and Nick got to know Dr. Peterson better, he began entertaining doubts about his faith. In some sense, he still sought to be a "Christian witness" and to share a message of repentance and trusting in Christ, but sometimes he got discouraged. Not only were there no "converts," but he also found it difficult to reconcile his beliefs with what he was learning in class. Gradually, as he talked less about Jesus and learned more about the unreliability of the Bible, he began to drift from the conservative faith he had grown up with.

One night at another of Jessica's parties, Nick drank a few more beers than he anticipated. Before long he was getting physical with Jessica. It started with grinding as they danced closely to an old Jay-Z song, then progressed to making out in the hot tub after some of the others had left. Three weeks and several dates later, he did something that would certainly disappoint his parents and former youth pastor if they found out. He lost his virginity. For most nineteen-year-olds, this might not have seemed like such a big deal, but for Nick it was huge. He was smitten with guilt and felt like he had turned against God. Years ago at a church youth conference Nick had pledged not to have sex until marriage, and now he had broken his word and violated his commitment.

Three

STRUGGLING WITH FAITH

THE FOLLOWING WEEK Nick called Duane, the youth pastor from his church back home. When Duane was leading Nick's accountability group the previous summer, Nick used to confess to him after missing a "quiet time" or struggling with lust.

"Duane, I need to talk to you about a couple things."

"Sure, Nick. What's up?"

"Duane, do you really believe the Bible we have today is true?"

"Of course, Nick."

"Why do you believe that?"

"Are you serious? The Bible is the most amazing book in the world. The Bible provides wisdom and my life is living proof that it's true."

Nick had heard this before and used to tell people the same thing.

"Yes, but how do you *know* it's reliable, Duane?"

"Don't you remember what I taught you during the summer? The Bible is true because of *faith*. Jesus said that without faith you'll never enter the kingdom of heaven. Regardless of circumstances, God's love is unchanging. You've got to just believe it and press on! Don't let the Devil pull you away, Nick!"

"Duane, I used to think that way, but lately I've had a lot of doubts. I've even reviewed the verses we learned last summer, but they don't mean anything. Dr. Peterson, my religion professor, has studied some of the oldest copies of the Bible available and he says there are hundreds of thousands of differences in the copies.[5] He also says there are other gospels written by people like Thomas, Mary, and Judas, and that most of Christianity is borrowed from pagan mythology. Do you know about all this?"

Duane didn't respond right away. "Nick, Christ hasn't called us to be perfect or to know all the answers. He calls us to be genuine and authentic. Keep trusting Him and He'll show you the way."

"Maybe you can pray for me, Duane. For the first several weeks I was here I felt like I was walking the narrow way, not drinking alcohol or looking at pornography, but recently

I've been doing both, and . . . well, I met this girl and spent more time with her than I should have."

"Did you sleep with her?"

Nick hesitated. "Well, not right away, but we sort of clicked and things went pretty fast and . . . I slept with her a couple days ago. I only did it once, and I feel really bad about it, but I'm also having some serious doubts, Duane."

"Nick, I'm sorry to hear that, but remember this—God loves you. I certainly don't know all the answers, but the Bible says that 'if we confess our sins, he is faithful and just and will forgive us our sins and purify us from all unright-eousness.'[6] I can tell you're struggling, so don't forget that God calls us to struggle *well*. We're not perfect; we need to confess our doubts and sins. You confessed it to me, and God will reward your honesty. If you feel tempted again, call me and we can pray together. Keep reading the Word, *by faith*, even if you don't understand! As a matter of fact, let's go to the Lord right now in prayer."

After Pastor Duane prayed, Nick felt encouraged and hoped he could press on in faith. He also decided his sexual mistake with Jessica wouldn't happen again, but that resolve was short-lived. In the weeks that followed, Nick found endless excuses to be alone with her, and several times they were sexually intimate again. Whatever guilty feelings he'd had at first were now being repressed, and it all seemed so good in a new sort of way. He had never known a girl so beautiful or felt such powerful longings. His drinking habits now included hard alcoholic beverages, and he drank on a regular basis with Jessica and their friends. Yet, even when consumed with Jessica on Saturday nights, he would occasionally attend the nearby Catalyst Fellowship Church on Sunday evenings. It made him feel better and gave him something spiritual to tell his parents when they called.

By November, Nick was agreeing more and more with Dr. Peterson's theological ideas and reading the Bible more critically, even when trying to draw inspiration from its words. He had always loved the poetry in Psalms, but as far as heeding any specific instructions or warnings in Scripture, Nick no longer felt the need to take such words literally. He acknowledged his rudeness to Dr. Peterson during the first weeks of class and Dr. Peterson reached out in kindness to Nick, answering all of his questions and bringing calm to any lingering confusion. He encouraged Nick in his academic potential and even had Nick and Jessica to the house for dinner so he and Mrs. Peterson could get to know them better.

During the Christmas holidays, Jessica stopped answering her cell phone. When she finally called back it was to break his heart by announcing that they should no longer be together. Nick grew depressed and his shattered faith endured another severe attack.

"Why, God? Why?" Nick prayed. "She was the first girl

I've really loved. Why did You let this happen to me? If You *are* real, why do You always mess up my life? Do You enjoy making me miserable?!"

Nick's parents were concerned about his depression *and* his walk with the Lord. His father was especially disturbed when he found Nick reading Bart Ehrman's book *Misquoting Jesus: The Story Behind Who Changed the Bible and Why.* But his father's concern was mild in comparison to the tears that filled his mother's eyes when Nick told her, "The Bible may be true for you, but it's not true for me."

Four

THE PROFESSED AGNOSTIC

BY LATE JANUARY, Nick was a professed agnostic —someone who *doesn't know* if God exists. Even though Nick couldn't agree with outright atheism, he felt betrayed by Christianity. For example, whenever he asked his pastor or parents questions about variances in the Bible, they had no answers. Not only could Dr. Peterson give good explanations, he took a personal interest in Nick, even inviting him over for dinner on several occasions.

Nick's pastor, who was always preaching about "community" and "authenticity," couldn't even remember Nick's name.

Nick had lots of questions. If God *did* exist, would He want us to believe a lie and just have blind faith? Nick's youth pastor liked to talk about how big God was. He always said that, as sinful human beings, we can't really know much on our own. *If we're so sinful and depraved in our knowledge,* Nick wondered, *how can my youth pastor be so certain in his knowledge? How can he know the Bible is the Word of God? And if God is so all-powerful, why doesn't He convince everyone that the Bible is true? Why so much confusion?*

Because of Dr. Peterson's friendship, effectiveness as a communicator, and competence in his subject matter, Nick enthusiastically enrolled in Peterson's Religious Textual Criticism course for the spring semester. One of the course requirements—a major twenty-page paper—excited Nick's imagination. He wanted to title his paper *The Plagiarism of the Bible: How the Bible Stole from Pagan Mythology,* so he stopped by Dr. Peterson's office to get his input. Walking in, he nearly collided with a tall and muscular African-American man who was just turning out the lights.

"Do you know if Dr. Peterson will be in his office today?" asked Nick.

"Actually, he's out all week. His sister had some sudden medical issues, so Dr. Peterson flew out to Oregon this morning and won't be back until Monday."

"Oh no, I'm so sorry to hear that," said Nick. "I hope it's not too serious."

The man nodded and waited for Nick to continue.

"My name is Nick. I'm taking Religious Textual Criticism this semester and I wanted to talk with Dr. Peterson about my research paper."

"Nice to meet you, Nick. I'm Jamal Washington, Dr. Peterson's new teaching assistant."

"Good to meet you," said Nick. "Wait—you're Jamal Washington? As in *the* Jamal Washington, former wide receiver for Notre Dame?"

Jamal laughed. "You certainly have a good memory."

"No way! I remember watching you on ESPN when I was in middle school! I wasn't a Notre Dame fan, but you were awesome! I was so frustrated when you separated your shoulder."

"That's nice of you," Jamal said with a smile. "At the time, I was pretty frustrated, too. One wrong move and there went my NFL dreams. I lived for football, but I think the Lord used that experience to help me focus more on Him and reevaluate my priorities."

Nick was surprised to learn Dr. Peterson's teaching assistant was a former football star. Though embarrassed to admit it, he couldn't picture a football player holding one of the most prestigious doctoral student scholarships on campus. Quickly shifting gears, he asked, "So Jamal, what have you been up to since you graduated from Notre Dame?"

"Well, let's see. I completed my four-year master's degree

at Dallas Theological Seminary, worked with one of my favorite professors in textual criticism, and spoke regularly at conferences. Lately I've been studying and researching the biblical manuscripts." Jamal paused, then said, "Nick, I'd like to hear about your paper, but I was just heading out for my morning caffeine. Do you have time to join me? We could discuss your ideas, and I'd like to hear your thoughts on textual criticism and the Bible."

"Sure, let's do it!" Nick couldn't believe it. He was about to have a religious conversation with a man who was once considered the nation's top wide receiver in college football.

Five

DID CHRISTIANITY BORROW FROM PAGAN MYTHOLOGY?

NICK WAITED for Jamal to down his first mouthful of coffee, then said, "I'm thinking about calling my paper *The Plagiarism of the Bible: How the Bible Stole from Pagan Mythology.*"

"Interesting," said Jamal. He took another swallow and then said, "I'm curious about one thing. What academic sources will you cite to document that the Bible stole from pagan mythology?"

"Um . . . I'm not sure. I haven't found any resources yet but it shouldn't be that hard. I read about it in one of Dan Brown's novels and saw a special on the History Channel. I also watched a YouTube video called . . ."

"Zeitgeist." Jamal chuckled as he finished Nick's sentence. "Nick, that sure is a popular video, especially in college dorms, but I would be careful about referring to it at the university. That video is considered a joke in academic circles. There are only a small handful of professors who still believe Christianity borrowed from pagan mythology, and nothing has been published academically on the subject recently. However," Jamal added with a slight grin, "if you could find *historical* documentation, that would make an excellent paper. Good luck!"

Nick wasn't sure what to say. "What do you mean?"

"Well, even in the most progressive circles of religious academia—in the Ivy League world for example—this idea of Christianity borrowing from pagan mythology is definitely not as popular as it once was. All we see now are novels and YouTube videos with zero historical documentation. *Academic* publishing houses are not publishing anything on the subject because there is simply no evidence."

"No evidence?" asked Nick.

"Nick, I've lectured on this subject to campus groups all across the country. Students are fascinated with it, and so they're naturally surprised when I quote Dr. J. Smith of the *Encyclopedia of Religion*, 'The category of dying and rising gods, once a major topic of scholarly investigation, must now be understood to have been largely a misnomer based on imaginative reconstructions and exceedingly late or highly ambiguous texts.'"[7]

Nick took a bite of his coffeecake.

"Let me explain in more detail. Dr. Greg Boyd, who earned his doctorate at Princeton Theological Seminary, and Dr. Paul Rhodes Eddy, who earned his doctorate at Marquette, agree with Smith. Hold on a second and I'll read you something from them." Jamal pulled out his Kindle and found the bookmarked page.

"Okay, here it is. 'The very category of ancient *dying and rising gods* has been called into question by most contemporary scholars. In short, when each of these myths is analyzed in detail, it turns out that either there is no actual death, no actual resurrection, or no actual *god* in the first place!'"[8]

"That's interesting," commented Nick as he sipped his coffee.

Jamal continued, "And even though in a few cases there were mere mentions of deaths, the resurrection was certainly not mentioned. One of the most popular skeptical books on this subject was written by Tim Callahan, editor of *Skeptic Magazine* and author of *The Secret Origins of the Bible*, and is more 'popular level' than academic." Jamal closed his Kindle and pulled out his computer. "Nick, I remember watching a video on Lee Strobel's *Faith Under Fire*[9] about this subject. Let me pull it up on the Internet and you can watch it. It's only a few minutes long."

Nick watched as Lee Strobel, a graduate of Yale University and former journalist with the *Chicago Tribune*, interviewed both Tim Callahan, religion editor of *Skeptic Magazine*, and Dr. Gary Habermas, who chairs the philosophy and theology department at Liberty University, and earned his two doctorates from Michigan State and Oxford:

STROBEL: Virtually all scholars agree that Jesus of Nazareth lived in the first century, preached about the kingdom of God, and was crucified. But what happened next is the most controversial issue of history. Did Jesus rise from the dead, and thus authenticate His claim to being the Son of God? Or is this the stuff of legend and mythology? For Christians, everything hinges on the resurrection.

Tim, let me start with you. In your book you suggest that the resurrection of Jesus isn't original at all, but it's merely a story that was recycled from earlier mythology and mystery religions. In your book you specifically mention the stories of Osiris, Odonis, and Attis. Can you explain what all this means?

CALLAHAN: Well, there were death and resurrection stories going all the way back as you said to Isis and Osiris, and usually Dionysus in Greek mythology became his own separate cult. In all of these they die an excruciating death of some sort—Dionysus is torn to pieces and eaten by the Titans—and then they rise physically from the dead.

HABERMAS: Let's take Odonis, probably the ancient god for which we have the clearest data that he was raised from the dead. We have four accounts that Odonis was raised. The earliest one is the second century AD. The other ones are between the second and fourth century AD. The earliest account we have for Attis is a third century AD. And while Isis and Osiris as a religion was definitely pre-Christian, there is no resurrection in Isis and Osiris. Osiris in particular is not raised.

STROBEL: Okay, Tim, how do you respond to that?

CALLAHAN: I would point out that often times the only copies of the myths we have are quite late as far as writings go but quite often we have some evidence of myths in the form of pictures on vases of the various mythic characters and the situations of the myths. So we're pretty sure that they were being told orally a lot earlier.

HABERMAS: If we're talking about stories on vases or in other reliefs there's still no resurrection. There are no resurrected gods for which we have data prior to the second century.

I've done a count recently of twelve hundred sources on the resurrection. Everything published since 1975 in German, French, and English, and I went back and I looked at how many of these scholars who hold university chairs for example, how many of them who are not Christians, who do not hold to the resurrection, how many of them would say that, in any way the mystery gods are a potential inspiration for Christianity, and I could count the number of skeptics on one hand. Out of twelve hundred scholars. It's a real minority.

CALLAHAN: Not entirely. I would still say that a common idea of a dying and a rising god was around before Jesus.

STROBEL: Well, that's not what Dr. Habermas has said.

CALLAHAN: Well, we would have to agree to disagree on that.

STROBEL: But one or the other of you isn't right.

HABERMAS: The point is, Tim, if you're going to hold to a dying and rising God before Jesus, I want to say where's the evidence?

CALLAHAN: Well, I would say that, first of all, that the myth of Dionysus probably does antedate Jesus, and yes, there isn't specifically a crucifixion, but I don't see that that's really that important a point. They all undergo a horrible, excruciating death.

HABERMAS: You're going to have to give me a date for the earliest inscription because Dionysus—I don't know anybody who thinks Dionysus is pre-Christian. Not the resurrection portion.

CALLAHAN: Okay, well, ah, all I can tell you is that the myth is that he is torn apart by the Titans, eaten and he is raised from the dead.

HABERMAS: But what's the date? What is the date?

CALLAHAN: I don't know the date of the original as far as any writings we have. With the myths, the Greek myths, most of our Greek myths we do have from later collections except we know they were told earlier because we have the vase paintings depicting them going way back in time.

HABERMAS: But the point, the question is, is there a resurrection? And since we don't have any resurrection

predating the second century, all the way to the fourth
century, are the earliest ones. Second to fourth we can
say, well maybe there's a resurrection there but there's
no data. There's absolutely no evidence for that position.

When the video ended, a strange mix of sensations was
brewing inside Nick. Admiration for a brilliant man who
had obviously done his homework in debating this attack
on Christianity, and frustration at the prospect of being
wrong about this.

Jamal broke into his thoughts. "So what do you think,
Nick?"

"I don't know. I haven't really researched any of this
yet."

Jamal looked at Nick, allowing him to digest what he
had just heard.

Nick continued, "But I thought Dr. Peterson mentioned
there was some truth to this."

Jamal smiled, wanting to be careful to demonstrate
both his respect for Dr. Peterson and his appreciation for the
full-ride scholarship and teaching assistantship Dr. Peterson had granted him. "You're right that he probably *mentioned* it, but I doubt he lectured on it extensively because
there simply isn't historical evidence for his belief. It's just
an opinion he has."

Nick was growing uneasy. Here was someone who not

only questioned Dr. Peterson's theory, but seemed intellectually capable of challenging it. Jamal's response was such a contrast to the simplistic answers his former Christian friends had given him.

As he wrestled through these thoughts, he decided to bring up another name mentioned in the *Zeitgeist* video. "Jamal, what about Mithras? I have heard more about Mithraism than any of the others and I didn't hear Callahan or Habermas talk about it. Did Mithraism exist?"

"Yes, Mithraism did exist.[10] But was Mithras called the 'Son of God' or the 'Light of the World'? No. I know of no such claims in the Mithraic literature. And the Mithraic scholar Richard Gordon says unequivocally that there is 'no death, burial, and resurrection of Mithras. None.'"[11]

Jamal continued, "The larger issue is the question of who influenced whom. With Christianity exploding onto the scene of the Roman Empire, it is evident that other religions adopted certain teachings and practices from Christianity in order to stem the tide of departing adherents or, perhaps, to attract Christians to their side.[12] The key is in the dating. According to available evidences, Mithraism did not gain a foothold in the Roman Empire until after AD 100.[13] M. J. Vermaseren, a specialist on the cult of Mithra, certifies that no Mithraic monument can be dated earlier than the end of the first century AD, and even the more extensive investigations at Pompeii, buried beneath the ashes of Vesuvius in AD 79, have not so far produced a single image of the god."[14]

Nick felt a migraine coming on, so he weakly thanked Jamal for sharing with him and headed back to his room. He was not only dealing with a lot of heavy-duty historical information, but his agnostic journey was being seriously challenged. His train had just left the station and already it was derailing. As if to punctuate that thought, his cell phone began vibrating as he trudged across campus. It jarred him out of his deep reflection, and the text he read startled him even more. *It was from Jessica.*

"Hey Nick! I was wondering if we could meet. I feel bad about how I treated you last month and I've really been missing you."

Six

A WALK ON KATY TRAIL

NICK AGREED to meet Jessica the next day. As he waited for her outside the campus Starbucks, memories brought him back to the night they met, their times of laughter and lively discussion, and their passion. When Jessica walked up they both smiled awkwardly. Entering the coffee shop, Nick took one look at all the students studying and felt it would be better if they went somewhere else.

"Hey Jess, this place is packed. Let's go walk Katy Trail. Do you have time for that?"

"Sure, we can order drinks and take them with."

Katy Trail had been a familiar running and biking place for Jessica and Nick, and memories of good times came easily. They weren't even five minutes into their walk when Jessica, fighting back tears, turned and said, "Nick, I've missed you so much. I was wrong. I should never have left you."

Not entirely surprised by this, Nick remained quiet. His mind was racing. *Is she manipulating me? Should we get back together? She sure does look good!*

"What happened between you and Allen?" he finally asked.

"Oh, he was too full of himself. I got tired of him telling me about his body-building and UFC events. One day I looked at his phone and found he was still talking regularly with his ex. Probably still sleeping with her. Jerk."

Still wrestling with what to think, Nick asked a sincere question. "Why did you leave me to begin with? Did I do something wrong? Or, were you interested in Allen all along?"

Jessica started tearing up again. "No, it was nothing you did, and it *wasn't* Allen."

Nick put his arm around her but didn't say anything. The truth is, he had doubts about both points. She was the one who had left him, not the other way around. *Does Jessica really miss me or is she just lonely?* He stopped walking and removed his arm. "Jessica, right now I can't get back with you like we were. I'm not even sure you really cared about me to begin with."

"Nick," she said, taking his hand and squeezing it. "I've always cared about you."

"Then why did you tell me we shouldn't be together? And what about Allen?" Nick let go of her hand. "Maybe we do care about each other at some level, but there are other things I'm dealing with right now."

"Like what?" Jessica said with that certain sarcasm in her voice Nick always resented.

"I'm wrestling with some spiritual issues."

"Oh, come on, Nick! Please don't tell me you're still obsessing over the Bible. I thought you'd given up on that!"

Nick frowned. "I did stop believing for a while, but now I'm not sure. I think the truth is pretty important."

"You're so indecisive, Nick."

"Look, Jessica, this matters to me. If you can't relate to that, you need to forget about me and move on with your life. I'm moving on with mine."

It was awkward and quiet on their way back to campus. After dropping Jessica off, Nick needed someone to call before he went out later that night.

"Hey Jamal, this is Nick. I know it's Friday and you probably have plans for the weekend, but I need to talk sometime soon. I'm wrestling with some serious spiritual questions about the Bible and I feel like it's affecting the way I live. Is there any way we can get together in the next few days?"

"Absolutely! Let's do it now. I'm actually over at Caruth Haven Coffee, hanging out with my friend Mina."

"Really? I don't want to interrupt time with your friend."

"Naw. She's real cool and quite a philosopher. She'll probably do better than me answering your questions. Come on over; we're here for another hour."

Seven

WHEN WAS THE BIBLE "PUT TOGETHER"?

"HEY, JAMAL!"

"Hi, Nick! This is Mina. She just graduated—with honors—from Rice University, and she's thinking about coming here to attend law school next year."

"Nice to meet you, Nick!"

Wow, she seems nice, thought Nick.

After some light conversation about law school and her home state of Arizona, Mina shifted the discussion. "Jamal mentioned that you two had an interesting conversation yesterday about the Bible."

"I'll say," replied Nick. "I was picking Jamal's brain about my *Religious Textual*

Criticism paper, and now I'm not sure what I should do. I was planning to write about how the Bible really isn't that unique, but after listening to Jamal, I'm having second thoughts."

"Interesting. Nick, what makes you think the Bible is not unique?"

"Well, because I've heard that the story of Jesus is nothing new. It's all borrowed from pagan mythology and has been applied to many different gods throughout history. Jesus is just the most recent version of the story. Plus, the Bible is full of mistakes from being copied so many times over the years, and there's no way to tell if it's accurate since we don't have the original documents."

Mina leaned forward. "Even scholars and critics who don't believe the Bible is historically accurate acknowledge there is a uniqueness to it. There is a similar theme of agreement running through the Bible's entirety, even though it was written over fifteen hundred years by more than forty authors."

Nick nodded. "I was telling Jamal there are lots of books and websites that say we have never had a definitive version of the Bible. Some authors suggest that Constantine mixed things up."

"Constantine had nothing to do with it," said Mina. "That's just Dan Brown fiction. I'm not sure what sites you are talking about, but keep in mind that 'facts' found on websites or in novels aren't necessarily true. When it comes to the Old Testament, the evidence clearly supports the position that the Hebrew Scriptures—as we know them today—were collected and recognized long before Constantine. Possibly as early as the fourth century BC, and certainly no later than 150 BC."

"Before Jesus?" asked Nick.

Mina nodded, "Yes, the last books recognized by the Jews as authoritative—as being written by true prophets of God—were Malachi, which was written around 450 to 430 BC, and Chronicles, which was written no later than 400 BC.[15] These books appear in the Greek translation of the Hebrew Scriptures, called the Septuagint, which was probably created between 250 and 150 BC.[16] In other words, the books of the Old Testament were collected and translated into Greek—not by the Vatican, not by Constantine, and not by the early Christians—but more than a hundred years before Jesus' birth as a result of the consensus of generations of Jewish rabbis and scholars. I'd say that's fairly definitive."[17]

"Wait a minute. How do you know so much?" asked Nick, feeling a little intimidated by her fluent articulation and natural authority on the subject.

Jamal cut in. "Nick, let me brag on Mina for a sec. She won the top philosophy of religion paper at Rice for an undergraduate student. She also received fellowship offers from Rutgers, New York University, and Notre Dame, but she's thinking about staying in Dallas to pursue law."

"Why would you do that, being such a philosopher?" asked Nick. "Why law?"

"I guess I got a little burned out. Studying analytic philosophy and debating religion is not my favorite thing in life. I'm not sure I want to spend the next five years studying philosophy. Maybe some day I'll move to New York and get my PhD, but now I'm thinking about becoming a lawyer here in Texas," replied Mina.

Nick could not forget his earlier conversation with Andrea. "Mina and Jamal, would you be open to meeting my friend Andrea? She used to be a Catholic, but after studying all this stuff that contradicts everything you've ever believed, she is full of questions. I have so many questions myself I don't know how to help her find answers."

"I'd love to meet her," said Mina.

Jamal nodded. "Hey, why don't the four of us meet here a week from today at 10:00 a.m.?"

"That sounds great, Jamal," replied Nick. "I'll see if I can get her to come."

Mina was scrolling through her calendar. "Good—I'm free too. Let's do it."

Eight

BART EHRMAN AND *MISQUOTING JESUS*

WHENEVER HE would talk with Mina and Jamal, Nick had a genuine interest in what they had to say, but he couldn't get past one obstacle. *How would Dr. Peterson respond? He must have known about Jamal's beliefs when he hired him as his teaching assistant.*

The following Monday Nick saw Dr. Peterson for the first time in a week.

"Well, it's wonderful to be back in class," said Dr. Peterson. "My sister has a tumor and is going through a series of medical tests, so my wife and I flew out to Oregon to be with her. We're hoping for the best. I appreciate all of your prayers and encouraging emails."

Prayers? Why would he thank us for our prayers if he doesn't believe in God? Nick wondered. *That's weird.*

"Today in class I want to begin sharing some observations in textual criticism that might challenge the way some of us were taught. The field of textual criticism has not always been as popular with the public as it is today. Bart Ehrman, of UNC Chapel Hill, gave it a real boost when he published his *New York Times* bestselling book, *Misquoting Jesus.*"

Over the break Nick had actually read that book, so he felt he might have an edge in this particular classroom discussion.

Peterson went on, "In the first chapter of his book, Bart recalled writing a paper while he was in seminary at Princeton. The paper dealt with a story in the second chapter of Mark[18] where some Pharisees angrily confronted Jesus and His disciples because they had been walking through the grain fields on the Sabbath, picking grains of wheat and eating them. Jesus responded by explaining to the Pharisees that 'the Sabbath was made for man, not man for the Sabbath.' He reminded the religious leaders that when David and his men were hungry, they went into the Temple 'when Abiathar was the high priest' and ate the showbread, which was restricted only for the priest to eat.[19] The well-known problem of this passage is that when one looks at the book of 1 Samuel, which Jesus is citing, it turns out that David did this not when Abiathar was the high priest, but when Abiathar's father *Ahimelech* was."

Dr. Peterson continued, "After Bart wrote the paper, his professor at Princeton made the suggestion, 'Maybe Mark just made a mistake.'[20] This is when Bart discovered that the Bible is not inerrant at all but contains mistakes."

Nick looked at the passage in the gospel of Mark, and then at the one in 1 Samuel. It seemed that what Peterson said was true. *Why did Pastor back home say that Scripture is the inerrant Word of God when it has mistakes like this one? I need to ask Jamal about this.*

Nick took notes on several other alleged variances mentioned by Dr. Peterson, carefully checking each one in his own Bible. Later that day he called Andrea to see if she was free to meet with Jamal and Mina on Friday. She seemed happy to be invited.

Nine

INERRANCY

JAMAL AND MINA were already there when Nick and Andrea arrived. After a few minutes of getting acquainted, Nick jumped right in. "Jamal, I have another question I hope you can help me with."

"Go ahead."

"Earlier this week Dr. Peterson brought up several passages of Scripture in which there are clear contradictions. Now, I remember my pastor back home always telling us the Bible is the inerrant Word of God. Do you believe that?"

Jamal smiled. "Good question. To begin with, I personally hold that the original words recorded by Paul, Mark,

John and the other biblical authors *are* the inerrant Word of God. What I *don't* believe is that God spoke in an audible voice to each author. Lewis Sperry Chafer, the founder and first president of Dallas Theological Seminary, put it well: 'Without violating the authors' personalities, they wrote with their own feelings, literary abilities, and concerns. But in the end, God could say, *That's exactly what I wanted to have written.*'"[21]

"But we don't have the original words that Paul, Mark, John, and the others recorded, right?" asked Andrea.

"Actually, we don't have the *originals* of any literature that old. That's why the question to ask is *can we reproduce the original to a high level of certainty?* The answer to that question is most definitely, yes! The ancient copies are *very* accurate even though there are some variances. Theologically, I believe the Bible is the inspired Word of God, and I personally believe in the inerrancy of Scripture because of the authority of the apostles and internal evidence of what Jesus said about it. I *also* accept that someone can be a Christian through faith in Christ's deity and resurrection without believing in inerrancy."

"But the Bible is a human book," Andrea said.

"You're absolutely right," said Mina. "The Bible *is* a human book, with human characteristics and about forty different human authors. But just because a book is written by humans doesn't mean it has errors."

"I don't believe that's true," Nick chimed in.

"Okay, check this out." Mina took out a piece of paper and started writing. She handed the paper to Nick, who read it aloud, "2+2=4, 4+4=8, 8+8=16."

"Where are the errors?" asked Mina.

Andrea didn't wait for Nick to answer, "There aren't any. But that's a bad illustration, because the Bible isn't a math book; there are mistakes in many of the parallel accounts."

"Remember, Andrea, when one claims inerrancy, that doesn't mean the copies we have today are inerrant, only the original. I'm claiming that God supernaturally used real human beings, some well-educated, like Isaiah and Luke, and others less so, to write His own thoughts—His Word— to communicate in a way that just about anyone could understand. If God *does* exist and can perform miracles, wouldn't you agree that God could, if He wanted to, communicate a message through ordinary people?"

"I'm not convinced," Andrea said.

"Nick?" Jamal asked.

"I'll have to think about it."

"Let me ask you two a real basic question," said Jamal. "Do you believe that God exists in reality?"

Ten

ANTI-SUPERNATURALISM

NICK WAS FIRST to answer. "I'm not sure what you mean."

Jamal continued, "Belief in God is a foundational truth that everyone must wrestle with. First of all, before even considering if God inspired a group of books and letters, a skeptic should ask if he is even open to the *possibility* of believing that God exists, assuming evidence is provided. Many of the professors in religious departments who deny that miracles happened or that God inspired the Bible are holding to an anti-supernatural bias. They hold to the philosophy of naturalism."

"Explain," said Nick.

"Well, someone who holds to a worldview of naturalism, atheism, or materialism believes there must be a naturalistic or materialistic explanation for everything. If God doesn't exist, then miracles don't exist either. But, if the worldview of naturalism is false and God *does* exist, then miracles are possible."

Nick nodded. "Okay, that makes sense."

"Let me ask you both a question. What is the greatest miracle ever described?"

"I don't know. The resurrection of Christ?" Andrea suggested.

"The resurrection of Christ is certainly a great miracle, but if you think about it, an even greater miracle would be the Creation. God creating the universe out of nothing. God speaking time, matter, space, and energy into existence. Now, if God *does* exist in reality, and created everything as we know it—all of the *water*, for instance—then it's not a problem for God to part the *waters* of the Red Sea, or for Jesus to turn *water* into wine, calm the *waters* of the storm, or walk on *water*. If the first miracle of Genesis 1:1 took place, then other miracles are possible, and through investigation I think we can discover that they are not only possible, but supported by historical evidence."

"I just don't know if I believe in miracles," commented Andrea. "I think Dr. Peterson's skepticism of the New

Testament is based on his academic scholarship, *not* a belief in magic."

Jamal reached for his backpack and pulled out his Kindle. "I have a good observation from Drs. Boyd and Eddy, two scholars I mentioned to Nick last week. They make the point that the anti-supernatural bias in some circles of New Testament scholarship is based on an unwarranted assumption. Let me read it to you."

> First, while every modern person of course grants that the world generally runs in accordance with natural laws, on what basis can anyone argue that it does so *exhaustively*—that is, without there ever being exceptions to these so-called laws? The absolute rejection of miracles isn't really a *conclusion* that is based on evidence or on reason—for neither evidence nor reason could warrant such an absolute conclusion. It is, rather, an *assumption*—a presupposition of the naturalistic worldview—pure and simple.[22]

"But there *are* laws of nature that are irrefutable," Andrea said.

"Boyd and Eddy address that issue as well," replied Jamal.

> Framing the issue in terms of "laws" has given some the impression that they are rules nature *must* obey—which is in part why many scholars conclude that miracles are impossible. . . . A natural law is a *description* of what we *generally* find in the world, not a *prescription* for what we *must* find in the world.[23]

Nick's frustration was growing. "Look. I've never even seen a miracle! Have you?"

"No I haven't," Jamal calmly responded. "Miracles are rare occurrences. But just because I haven't experienced one does not invalidate other people's claims."

"But you did admit that miracles are rare."

"Yes, they are rare. I too am sometimes skeptical when I hear claims of specific, physical healing, or of former Muslims seeing visions of Jesus, especially when the messenger is overly emotional or dramatic. But the point is—just because an event is rare or happens only once doesn't mean we should absolutely believe it's impossible."

"Mina," Andrea put in, "David Hume indicated that it was wiser to place faith in regular and natural events rather than rare events that only take place once."

Mina smiled. "Yes, Hume was a naturalistic. Yet, consider all the rare events we believe in that happened only once. Probably the best example would be *you*—a distinct entity with no exact duplicate in the world. Your very existence goes against probability, and only happened once, but I still believe in this rare event. Don't you?"

"Of course," Andrea said.

"How do you even know this God who supposedly created the universe and inspired the Bible actually exists?" Nick asked, trying to answer some basic question lurking in his mind.

Mina continued, "There are multiple reasons why I believe faith in God's existence is logical and probable. For example, my conscience bears witness to a moral law or rule of decent behavior we all believe in. For example, around the world, people hold to the principles of love, kindness, courage, and 'do unto others as you would have them do unto you.' Now, I know many atheists who believe in these principles too, but I don't think they have any basis for explaining why these moral laws exist. We can't scientifically test if an action is always loving or unloving, but we can see the fruit of love, particular acts of love, and will have little doubt of the reality of love when we see certain positive actions. Because I believe that objective moral laws exist, I also believe that an objective moral lawgiver must exist, who transcends us and provides the standard of what is right, good, just, loving, and fair. This being is who I call 'God.'"

"Okay, I see your point," said Nick. "Maybe God's existence is possible, but I still have doubts about Scripture. How do we really know that what we have today is what was written down?"

"Hang on a minute—someone keeps calling me." Jamal pulled out his phone and saw that he'd missed several calls from Dr. Peterson.

Eleven

JAMAL'S HELP

"**HI, JAMAL,** this is Bill. I need a doctoral fellow to finish teaching two of my classes and I would like to give you the opportunity. We'll provide an extra stipend and reward an additional six hours toward your doctorate studies. I know it's last minute, but we learned that my sister's cancer is malignant, and I've decided to take a leave of absence to spend time with her. President Rutgers thinks it's a good idea and I assured him my classes would be in good hands. All right, Jamal, we're getting ready to board the plane to Oregon. Please call me back when you get a chance."

As Jamal prayed silently for the healing

of Dr. Peterson's sister, he sensed the Holy Spirit reminding him of his devastating injury at Notre Dame four years ago, and the way he had prayed then . . .

Dear Heavenly Father, I pray that You would heal my shoulder. Lord, You said we needed the faith of a mustard seed to move mountains, but I also know that You said Your "grace is sufficient." Lord, You know the doctor's report isn't good, but You're sovereign. God, sometimes I've lived for my glory rather than Yours. I have faith that You can heal me, but You know what's best. May You be glorified either way. If I lose my opportunity to shine for You on the field this year, I pray that You will open other doors so I can serve You and share Your message with the world. Amen.

Jamal did not want to delay his response, so he found Dr. Peterson's number and dialed.

"Hello?"

"Dr. Peterson, this is Jamal. My prayers are going with you as you visit your sister, and I'm honored to help teach your courses."

"Thanks, Jamal. I appreciate you and I know you'll do an excellent job. You have two master's degrees and you know your stuff. Just teach about the ancient manuscripts."

"You understand that my conclusions about the manuscripts are different than yours, right?"

"Oh yes, you are more evangelical and agree with my mentor, Bruce Metzger, at Princeton. That's quite all right,

Jamal. I trust you. You have the syllabus, so be yourself and teach the course. Don't hesitate to call me if you need anything."

"Thank you, Dr. Peterson. I'll give it my very best."

"I'll be checking my email every morning, so please keep in touch so I can help you as needed."

Twelve

WHEN WAS THE NEW TESTAMENT WRITTEN?

"GOOD MORNING, class. As most of you read in your email, Dr. Peterson is taking the rest of the semester off and has asked me to finish teaching the course. Your reading assignments and paper requirements will stay the same, and we'll continue reading about the manuscripts of ancient religious literature. Today we're again looking at the New Testament." Jamal started clicking through his PowerPoint presentations and pulled out several sheets of ancient-looking paper before beginning his lecture.

"Class, what I'm passing around today are pieces of papyrus."

Nick glanced at Jamal's first PowerPoint slide, which read *When Was the New Testament Written?*

Jamal walked across the front of the room as he taught. "The original documents, what scholars call the *autographs* of the books in the New Testament—the writings of Matthew, Mark, Luke, John, Paul, Jude, James, and Peter—disintegrated over time. Fortunately, we have many manuscript copies, close to the original and written in Greek. In the twentieth century, archaeological discoveries confirmed the accuracy of the New Testament manuscripts. The type of paper you are holding is what the earliest copies were written on."

Nick was curious where this lecture was going. Jamal flipped to the next slide and continued, "This is a picture of the John Rylands manuscript dating back to AD 130. Next is the Chester Beatty Papyri, dating AD 155, and the Bodmer Papyri II, dating AD 200. Because there are multiple papyri, and there is strong internal evidence within these writings, research indicates that all of these texts were written before AD 80."

At this moment, a girl in the front row raised her hand. "Mr. Washington, I thought Dr. Peterson believed that the manuscripts were written much later."

"Do you remember the dates he gave? And what books he was speaking of specifically?"

"No."

"Well, I've read most of Dr. Peterson's works. While he does agree with the early dating of Paul, he believes the gospels were written later. However, he hasn't written extensively on providing a case for the later dating."

"Why should we believe you?" interrupted another girl sitting beside her friend.

"Good question, Lynne. I appreciate your search for truth. In my next slides, I have documented the historical evidence from leading scholars. All of this is online and you can download and study the evidence yourself. Let me begin with this thought in regard to the papyrus manuscripts from Dr. Millar Burrows, who for many years was a professor of biblical theology at Yale Divinity School.

> Another result of comparing New Testament Greek with the language of papyri [discoveries] is an increase of confidence in the accurate transmission of the text of the New Testament itself.[24]

"I'll continue to the next scholar, William F. Albright, who was deemed the world's foremost biblical archaeologist."

> We can already say emphatically that there is no longer any solid basis for dating any book of the New Testament after about AD 80, two full

generations before the date between 130 and 150 given by the more radical New Testament critics of today.[25]

I guess Dr. Peterson would be a "radical New Testament critic" according to this William F. Albright, Nick thought.

Jamal continued, "Sir William Ramsay, one of the greatest archaeologists ever to have lived, was a student of the German historical school, which taught that the book of Acts was a product of the mid-second century AD and not of the first century as it purports to be. After reading modern criticism about the book of Acts, Ramsay became convinced that it was not a trustworthy account of the facts of its time (AD 50) and therefore was unworthy of consideration by a historian. So in his research on the history of Asia Minor, Ramsay paid little attention to the New Testament. His investigation, however, eventually compelled him to consider the writings of Luke, the author of the book of Acts. As an archaeologist, he observed the meticulous accuracy of the historical details and gradually his attitude toward the book of Acts began to change.[26] He was forced to conclude that 'Luke is a historian of first rank. . . . This author should be placed along with the very greatest of historians.'"[27]

Nick raised his hand.

"Yes, Nick," Jamal said.

"Okay. I have a question. This may seem stupid, but what historical details would lead this Sir William Ramsay to believe that Luke was a 'first rank' historian? My pastor back home taught on Luke for a year and I don't remember him ever mentioning anything that sounded remotely historical. Mostly he talked about our relationship with Christ and what was wrong with the Pharisees. How do we know Luke's writing is historical?"

"That's not a bad question, Nick. Many popular ministers have been so dedicated to the *application* of the text to one's personal life that the *historical* elements are missed. However, many scholars have written on the historical accuracy of The Acts of the Apostles. For example, Colin Hemer, a classical scholar and historian, documents eighty-four facts in the last sixteen chapters of Acts that have been confirmed by historical and archaeological research.[28] If you give me a second, I will pull up a list of details that Luke accurately records."

Nick raised his hand again.

"Go ahead, Nick."

"Mr. Washington, how would Luke's naming of historical data indicate that he was writing the material in his lifetime? Historians and novelists regularly include documentation and correct geographical details without living in the same time period. Correct historical documentation doesn't necessarily prove Luke's authenticity."

"Nick, it does in Luke's case for several reasons. For one, Luke did not have access to advanced nautical charts or modern maps like we have today. He couldn't just pull up Google on his iPhone and look these things up. Second, at the end of the book of Acts the main character in the story, Paul, is still alive. Now, if you found a biography of John F. Kennedy in which the story abruptly ended with no mention of his death, it's very likely that you'd find it was written sometime before his death. Not definitely, but it's certainly more likely. Also, we have Ignatius and Polycarp quoting the book of Acts around 107 and 110 AD, indicating that Luke's book had to be not only written but widely circulated before then. Let me show you several examples on these PowerPoint slides that provide archeological evidence confirming Luke's accuracy."

Jamal clicked through several slides, and then paused on one. "In the book of Acts,[29] *politarch* are the civil authorities of Thessalonica. For years, many German scholars and critics were adamant that there was no such title as 'politarch.' Sir William Ramsay, the world's authority in this era of archeology, believed that too until he discovered . . ."

. . . nineteen inscriptions have been found that use the term *politarch*. Five of those inscriptions are in reference to Thessalonica.[30]

Jamal glanced up at the screen and then back to his students. "After investigating the evidence, Dr. Ramsay considered how someone writing in the second century could be so accurate about intricate details specifically correlating to the *first* century. Sir Ramsay was forced to conclude that Acts had to be a first-century document and therefore reliable about the details of the first century."[31]

Jamal clicked through another slide as he continued talking. "Another term used by Luke that critics were skeptical of was *Asiarch*.[32] Look up on the screen at Luke's reference in Acts 19:31.

> Even some of the officials of the province, friends of Paul, sent him a message begging him not to venture into the theater.

"Students," Jamal said, "Dr. Ramsay discovered in his research that his previous assumptions were false because other ancient writers, like Strabo, speak of these officials who were chosen from the wealthiest and most aristocratic in the province. Here's Luke 3:1.

> In the fifteenth year of the reign of Tiberius Caesar—when Pontius Pilate was governor of Judea, Herod tetrarch of Galilee, his brother

> Philip tetrarch of Iturea and Traconitis, and Lysanias tetrarch of Abilene—

"Once again, as a skeptic, Sir Ramsay thought this must be an inaccuracy on Luke's part since the only Lysanias previously known had been killed in 36 BC. However . . .

> An inscription dated between AD 14 and 29 was found near Damascus, confirming the existence of a first century "Lysanias the tetrarch."[33]

"Ramsay pondered, 'How could Luke be so accurate about such details if he was writing in the second century?' Again the scholars were proven wrong and Luke right."

I need to reread the books of Luke and Acts, Nick thought. *I never knew there were so many historical facts in what he was saying.*

When class was over, Nick called Andrea. "You've got to hear what Jamal was teaching in class. I never knew there was so much history in the New Testament."

"Nick, it sounds like you're starting to agree with him."

"I'm not sure yet, but he seems to know what he's talking about. His open office hours are at two o'clock. Let's go see him."

Thirteen

THE BIBLIOGRAPHICAL TEST

"NICK AND ANDREA! Come on in," said Jamal.

"Thanks, Mr. Washington. Hey, we were . . ."

"Hold on a minute. *Mr. Washington?*"

"Oh—sorry, Jamal. I was just telling Andrea about your class and we wondered if you had a few minutes so we could pick your brain about a couple things."

"Absolutely. Have a seat. What are your questions?" asked Jamal.

Andrea spoke first. "Well, Nick was telling me you implied the New Testament is historically accurate. I used to believe that, but not anymore. How can we possibly know that what we read in the

Bible today is exactly what was originally written down?"

"That's pretty easy. There are a couple of tests that historians use. The first is the bibliographical test."

"As in *bibliography*?" asked Nick.

"No, the word is biblio*graphical*. The bibliographical test is an examination of the textual transmission by which ancient documents reach us from the past. In other words, since we don't have the original manuscripts, the bibliographical test answers questions like: How reliable are the copies we have? How many manuscripts have survived? How consistent are they? What is the time interval between the original and the existing copies?"[34]

"Wait a second," said Andrea. "Is this bibliographical test true for all other historical works besides the Bible?"

"Absolutely. Let's take the history of Thucydides, from 460 to 400 BC. His work is available to us from only eight manuscripts dated about AD 900, nearly thirteen hundred years after he wrote. The manuscripts of the history of Herodotus are likewise late and scarce. Let me read to you from F. F. Bruce, who was the Rylands Professor of Biblical Criticism and Exegesis at the University of Manchester."[35]

Jamal spun his chair around and plucked a book off the shelf. Flipping through the pages he found what he was looking for. "Listen to this, Andrea. F. F. Bruce wrote,"

No classical scholar would listen to an argument that

the authenticity of Herodotus or Thucydides is in doubt because the earliest manuscripts of their works which are of use to us are over 1,300 years later than the originals.[36]

"What about more familiar classical works—like Aristotle?" asked Andrea.

"Good question. Aristotle wrote his *Poetics* around 343 BC, yet the earliest copy we have is dated AD 1100—a gap of nearly fourteen hundred years—and only forty-nine copies, or manuscripts, exist. Caesar composed his history of the *Gallic Wars* between 58 and 50 BC, and its manuscript authority rests on only nine or ten copies dating back to a thousand years after his death."[37]

"Whoa . . . how do you know all this?" asked Nick.

"I've researched it extensively. For one whole semester during seminary I taught at a private Catholic high school. I had to deliver the same lecture for three sections and I still have most of it memorized." Jamal stood up and grabbed another book off the shelf. "Let me read to you from Dr. Bruce Metzger, who was the author or editor of fifty books on the manuscript authority of the New Testament as well as other first-century classics. Many consider him to have been the foremost manuscript authority in the world. Incidentally, he was also Dr. Peterson's mentor at Princeton. Let me read what Dr. Metzger concluded."

Consider Tacitus, the Roman historian who wrote his *Annals of Imperial Rome* in about A.D. 116. His first six books exist today in only one manuscript, and it was copied about A.D. 850. Books eleven through sixteen are in another manuscript dating from the eleventh century. Books seven through ten are lost. So there is a long gap between the time that Tacitus sought his information and wrote it down and the only existing copies.

With regard to the first-century historian Josephus, we have nine Greek manuscripts of his work *The Jewish War*, and these copies were written in the tenth, eleventh, and twelfth centuries. There is a Latin translation from the fourth century and medieval Russian materials from the eleventh or twelfth century.[38]

Jamal looked up before continuing. "Now listen carefully to what he says next."

The quantity of New Testament material is almost embarrassing in comparison with other works of antiquity.[39]

"Why is it embarrassing?" Andrea asked.

Jamal leaned in as if to share some secret information. "Andrea, with the New Testament, scholars have documented more than 5,600 Greek copies, excluding thousands of Latin manuscripts.

"One of my former professors, Dr. Daniel Wallace, is one of the leading experts in textual criticism. His textbook on Greek is used by the majority of schools that teach intermediate Greek, including Yale Divinity School, Princeton Theological Seminary, and Cambridge University. He said there have been many more recent discoveries. Well over two hundred biblical manuscripts, ninety of which are in the New Testament, were discovered in Sinai in 1975 when a hidden compartment of St. George's Tower was uncovered. Dr. Wallace has observed that recent discoveries all confirm the transmission of the New Testament has been accomplished in relative purity, and that God has preserved the text from destruction. In addition to the manuscripts, there are 50,000 fragments sealed in boxes. Almost thirty separate New Testament manuscripts have been identified; Wallace and other scholars believe that there may be many more."[40]

"Why haven't we heard all this before?" asked Andrea.

"Well, many of these discoveries are very recent. You can read about all this online at The Center for the Study of New Testament Manuscripts, led by Dr. Wallace. Check out his website, www.csntm.org. Wallace and his team of scholars have been endorsed by some of the leading universities around the world, including the University of Cambridge, the University of Leeds, the University of St. Andrews, and the University of Edinburgh.

"Dr. Wallace has personally studied ancient manuscripts by visiting the Vatican, Cambridge University, Mount Sinai, Istanbul, Florence, Berlin, Dresden, Munster, Cologne, Patmos, and Jerusalem, and he strongly affirms that recent discoveries have helped reveal the overwhelming reliability of the New Testament."[41]

"Jamal, can you clarify something for me?" said Andrea.

"Sure."

"I know you just said this, but how many New Testament manuscripts exist today?" asked Andrea.

"Thousands. Over 5,600 Greek manuscripts are catalogued, but Wallace and his team are consistently putting more up on their website. If you go beyond the Greek manuscripts and consider all the copies of the Latin Vulgate and other translations, that number approaches 24,000."

"So," said Nick. "According to Metzger and Wallace and other scholars, there is an abundance of Bible manuscripts, but with others like Herodotus, Aristotle, and Thucydides, there are only a few copies."

"That's correct, Nick."

No one spoke for several moments, and then Jamal grinned. "Okay, you've been asking me questions since the minute you walked in. Now it's my turn. What classical work comes second to the New Testament in manuscript authority?"

"I have no idea," Andrea admitted.

"Nick?"

"Beats me."

"Homer's *Iliad*," responded Jamal. "It has 643 catalogued, discovered manuscripts."

"That would make sense," commented Andrea. "I remember Plato recording that all philosophers had the need to respond to Homer."

"Wait a minute," said Nick. "That doesn't mean everything Homer recorded was true, right?"

"Of course not! Manuscript authority simply tells us that what we have today is what was originally written down. Take the manuscripts of Homer's works. They tell us we can know with about ninety-five percent certainty this is what Homer actually wrote. That doesn't mean the details of Achilles being shot in the heel or the Greeks concealing themselves in the Trojan Horse were historically true. Homer could have made some of it up in his artistic poetry. Manuscript authority only tells us that today's copies are close to the original."

"Interesting," said Nick.

"Nick and Andrea, I have another observation from Dr. Craig Blomberg, former senior research fellow at Cambridge University in England and current professor of New Testament at Denver Seminary. Blomberg explains that the texts of the New Testament 'have been preserved in far greater number and with much more care than have any other ancient documents.' He concludes that '97–99 percent of the New Testament can be reconstructed beyond any reasonable doubt.' "[42]

"That's a pretty high percentage, but Blomberg is still admitting the possibility of error," commented Andrea.

"Blomberg is not admitting error in the original, but that there could be some variance in the copies you and I have. However—and this is a crucial point—within the variants in the copies, not one variant covers *major* doctrinal issues."

Jamal glanced at his watch. "Nick and Andrea, I'm glad you came by. Right now I need to pull a few things together in order to teach my next class, but we'll actually be covering the issue of variants in class on Wednesday. Andrea, you're welcome to sit in if you have the time."

"Thanks, Jamal," said Andrea.

As they left, Nick asked, "Think you'll come to class next Wednesday?"

"Sure. I'll stop by."

Fourteen

WHAT ABOUT THE "MISTAKES" IN THE BIBLE?

WITHIN TWO DAYS of Jamal's first lecture, word had spread like wildfire among the Religious Studies Department that Jamal had provided a case that the New Testament was historically accurate. Many of the faculty disagreed with Jamal's viewpoint, but didn't seem too concerned because most had encountered conservative theology with visiting professors from the University of Dallas and Dallas Theological Seminary. Besides, one of their former faculty members, Dr. Clayton Ingraham, was now covering Dr. Peterson's Introduction to Religion class. Ingraham and Peterson had been best of friends in former years and Ingraham promised to keep an eye on Jamal while Peterson was gone.

Meanwhile, Nick was so enthusiastic about Jamal's lecture he not only invited Andrea, but also Jamal's friend Mina, several guys from his floor, and—on a whim—Jessica.

When Nick showed up to class, he saw Andrea and Mina sitting together in the back row with Jessica just a few chairs over. Nick first went over and talked with the three girls, then walked to the front of the room to tell Jamal about the visitors he'd invited. The classroom was more like a small auditorium seating about one hundred and fifty people, and Jamal was busy setting up his PowerPoint presentation. As he glanced back to where the girls were seated he noticed Dr. Ingraham sitting at the end of the row with his arms crossed. "It's good to see you, Dr. Ingraham," he said over the noise of students finding their seats. "Thanks for joining our class."

"Jamal," Dr. Ingraham said with a nod, but no smile. He didn't say, "Hi, Jamal" or "Thanks," just, "Jamal," as if irritated or not wanting to get too personal.

"All right, class, let's begin," said Jamal. "We'll start with a quick review of our last session. In what century was the New Testament written? Who remembers? Yes, Lynne."

"The first century."

"That's correct. Now, from your notes based on my PowerPoint, give one of the evidences that Millar Burrows of Yale said 'provides confidence in the accurate transmission of the text of the New Testament.' Go ahead, Craig."

"The discoveries of the papyri copies," said Craig.

"Good," Jamal responded.

There was a noticeable clearing of the throat toward the back of the room. "Pardon my interruption, class, but Instructor Washington, who has not yet earned his PhD, seems to be teaching Christian fundamentalism rather than verifiable truth," Dr. Ingraham said in a loud voice.

The class awkwardly fell quiet as every student turned to see who was interrupting. *What in the world is Clayton doing?* Jamal thought to himself.

Nick felt his heart sink, thinking he should have never invited friends to join him.

"Just make sure you tell these students about the variants in the papyri," Ingraham continued.

"As a matter of fact, Dr. Ingraham, we'll be covering that very topic today," Jamal calmly replied. "Why don't you hear me out, and if you still have questions, perhaps we can talk privately afterwards." Jamal was not about to be derailed from his lecture.

"Class, Dr. Ingraham is referring to the variants found in the papyri. A textual variant is any instance where the New Testament manuscripts have alternative wordings. According to Dr. Bart Ehrman of Chapel Hill, there are between 300,000 and 400,000 variants among New Testament manuscripts. Given that the Greek New Testament of today has roughly 138,000 words, the idea that there are two to three times as many variants as words might seem quite disturbing. The truth, however, is that the large number of variants is a direct result of the extremely large number of New Testament manuscripts available. The more manuscripts you possess, the more variants; the fewer the manuscripts, the fewer the variants. But this is not the whole picture. When the variants are looked at more closely, here's what we see."[43]

Jamal clicked through another slide as he continued lecturing. "By far the most significant category of variants is spelling differences. The name John, for example, may be spelled with one *n* or with two. Clearly, a variation of this sort in no way jeopardizes the meaning of the text. Spelling differences account for roughly seventy-five percent of all variants.[44] That's between 225,000 and 300,000 of all the variants! Another large category of variants consists of the synonyms used across manuscripts. For instance, some manuscripts may refer to Jesus by His proper name, while others may say, 'Lord' or 'He.' Such differences hardly call the meaning of the text into question."[45]

Nick began to smile as he glanced around the room. Dr. Ingraham probably hadn't expected Jamal's quick and intelligent response.

"Now take a look at this slide." Jamal glanced at the screen, then continued, "As Drs. Norm Geisler and Frank

Turek say,

> The process of comparing the many copies and quotations allows an extremely accurate reconstruction of the original even if errors were made during copying. How does this work? Consider the following example. Suppose we have four different manuscripts that have four different errors in the same verse, such as Philippians 4:13 ("I can do all things through Christ who gives me strength."). Here are the hypothetical copies:
>
> I can do all t#ings through Christ who gives me strength.
>
> I can do all th#ngs through Christ who gives me strength.
>
> I can do all thi#gs through Christ who gives me strength.
>
> I can do all thin#s through Christ who gives me strength.
>
> Is there any mystery what the original said? None whatsoever. By the process of comparing and cross-checking, the original New Testament can be reconstructed with great accuracy.[46]

"When all variations are considered, only about one percent involve the meaning of the text. One percent! But even this fact can be overstated. For instance, there is disagreement about whether 1 John 1:4 should be translated, 'Thus we are writing these things so that *our* joy may be complete' or 'Thus we are writing these things so that *your* joy may be complete.' While this disagreement does involve the meaning of the passage, it in no way jeopardizes a central doctrine of the Christian faith. This is why the authors of *Reinventing Jesus* conclude, "The short answer to the question of what theological truths are at stake in these variants is—none."[47]

Fifteen

THE INTERNAL EVIDENCE TEST

"ARE THERE ANY questions?" asked Instructor Washington.

Nick glanced at Dr. Ingraham, but Ingraham was merely watching Jamal without expression.

"Yes, Andrea," Jamal called out.

"Hi . . . thanks. Just because we have an abundance of manuscript authority doesn't mean everything that Paul, Matthew, Luke, and the others wrote is necessarily true. You mentioned the other day that, even though we have over six hundred copies of Homer's *Iliad*, we don't need to believe everything he wrote. For example, Achilles being shot in his heel with an arrow, or the Greeks hiding in the Trojan horse. Can you explain that some more?"

"You're right, Andrea. The bibliographical test determines only that the text we have now is what was originally recorded.[48] That's why we're about to address *internal criticism*. During our last class I mentioned that we can believe in the historical detail because of the internal evidence. As an example, I showed documentation of eighty-four historical details confirmed in the book of Acts, written by Luke to Theophilus.

"Years ago I attended a seminar in northern Virginia led by John Warwick Montgomery, who has over a dozen earned degrees, including three doctorates. He wrote:

> Historical and literary scholarship continues to follow Aristotle's eminently just dictum that the benefit of doubt is to be given to the document itself, not arrogated by the critic to himself. . . . This means that one must listen to the claims of the document under analysis, and not assume fraud or error unless the author disqualifies himself by contradictions or known factual inaccuracies.[49]

"Now, I don't have time to go over all of the details of Acts like I did last class, but let me flip over a few slides to Luke's first book that we didn't even cover. Let's read the first four verses of the gospel of Luke.

> Inasmuch as many have undertaken to compile a narrative of the things that have been accomplished among us, just as those who from the beginning were eyewitnesses and ministers of the word have delivered them to us, it seemed good to me also, having followed all things closely for some time past, to write an orderly account for you, most excellent Theophilus, that you may have certainty concerning the things you have been taught. (Luke 1:1–4 ESV)

"Andrea, multiple scholars acknowledge Luke's historical accuracy. For example, this slide has the conclusion of Dr. John McRay, professor of New Testament and archaeology at Wheaton College, speaking of Luke, the physician and historian.

> He's erudite, he's eloquent, his Greek approaches classical quality, he writes as an educated man, and archaeological discoveries are showing over and over again that Luke is accurate in what he has to say.[50]

"Other writers of the New Testament also claimed careful investigation or eyewitness testimony. Who has a Bible with them?" No one moved. "Come on, guys, the Bible is a required text for this class."

Nick reached down, pulled a small red Bible out of his backpack, and waved it at Jamal.

"Okay, good. Nick, read 2 Peter 1:16–17 and tell us what Peter has to say."

As usual, Nick began more loudly than he had planned. "For we were not making up clever stories when we told you about the powerful coming of our Lord Jesus Christ. We saw his majestic splendor with our own eyes when he received honor and glory from God the Father. The voice from the majestic glory of God said to him, 'This is my dearly loved Son, who brings me great joy.'"[51]

"Thanks, Nick. So what do you observe in the text that Nick just read? Yes, Mike?"

"It seems that Peter and his audience were familiar with the myths that were circulating, but Peter wanted to make a clear distinction by providing testimony of being an eyewitness of Christ," said Mike.

"Good. Now, why don't you read to us from John 19:35."

Mike borrowed a Bible from the girl next to him and read, "This report is from an eyewitness giving an accurate account. He speaks the truth so that you also can believe."[52]

"Thank you, Mike. Now, let's review what we learned

both this morning and earlier this week. First, the bibliographical test confirms that the New Testament we read today accurately represents what was originally written. Second, the internal evidence test reveals individual authors of individual books claiming to be eyewitnesses or to have carefully investigated the truth."

Nick looked back and noticed that both Andrea and Jessica seemed interested. Jessica caught his eye and flashed a smile. And then Dr. Ingraham spoke up again. "Mr. Washington! There are lots of popular religious books by Joseph Smith, Muhammad, and others who claim to be eyewitnesses and inspired by God, but that doesn't make their writings true."

Sixteen

JOSEPH SMITH, MUHAMMAD, AND OTHER TRUTH CLAIMS

"YES, DR. INGRAHAM, many people have claimed to be eyewitnesses, but as we discussed earlier, the New Testament accounts of Christ were circulated during the lives of His contemporaries. These people, whose lives overlapped His, could certainly confirm or deny the accuracy of the accounts. Even when confronted by the most severe opponents, the New Testament writers appealed to common knowledge concerning Jesus. Class,

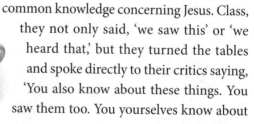

they not only said, 'we saw this' or 'we heard that,' but they turned the tables and spoke directly to their critics saying, 'You also know about these things. You saw them too. You yourselves know about it.' Now class, does anyone know of a specific passage in which we see this?"[53]

The class was silent.

"Okay, Mina, I see you smiling. Today we have a few visitors with us, and one of them is a friend of mine who graduated from Rice. She wrote an award-winning paper on this very subject. Why don't you share a couple passages that come to mind, Mina."

"Sure. In Acts 2:22, Peter says, 'Men of Israel, listen to these words: Jesus the Nazarene, a man attested to you by God with miracles and wonders and signs which God performed through Him in your midst, just as you yourselves know . . .'[54]

"Another one of my favorites is Acts 26:24–26," Mina continued. "'Suddenly, Festus shouted, "Paul, you are insane. Too much study has made you crazy!" But Paul replied, "I am not insane, Most Excellent Festus. What I am saying is the sober truth. And King Agrippa knows about these things. I speak boldly, for I am sure these events are all familiar to him, for they were not done in a corner!"'"[55]

"Did you hear that?" asked Jamal. "One had better be careful when he says to his opposition, 'You know this also,' because if there isn't common knowledge and agreement on the details, the challenge will be shoved right back down his throat."[56]

Good point. This must be embarrassing for Dr. Ingraham,

Nick thought. *But Lord, this is embarrassing for me! I acted just like Clayton Ingraham when I talked to my parents over Christmas.*

Jamal continued lecturing, "F. F. Bruce, who was a foremost authority of ancient biblical literature at the University of Manchester, explained about the primary-source value of the New Testament.

> It was not only friendly eyewitnesses that the early preachers had to reckon with; there were others less well disposed who were also conversant with the main facts of the ministry and death of Jesus. The disciples could not afford to risk inaccuracies (not to speak of willful manipulation of the facts), which would at once be exposed by those who would be only too glad to do so. On the contrary, one of the strong points in the original preaching is the confident appeal to the knowledge of the hearers; they not only said, "We are witnesses of these things," but also, "As you yourselves also know" (Acts 2:22). Had there been any tendency to depart from the facts in any material respect, the possible presence of hostile witnesses in the audience would have served as a further corrective.[57]

"So if we have evidence that suggests the New Testament we read today is a reliable and trustworthy copy of the original, and we have reason to believe the original was an accurate representation of what Jesus Christ and His early followers said and did, what choices are we faced with as we read the biblical text?" Jamal paused to glance around the room, then said, "Well, class, it's time to finish things up. Does anyone have any questions?"

"I don't have any questions," said Dr. Ingraham. "But I would like to make a comment. You have clearly done your research and have given me some things to consider. I apologize for interrupting your lecture. Class, I apologize to you as well. Your instructor has done a very good job today."

At this, the class broke out in applause and the momentum seemed to shift in Jamal's favor. Nick looked to where Andrea and Jessica were sitting and caught smiles from both. Though he returned their smiles, his insides were churning. Intellectually, he was being convinced that the New Testament was trustworthy and historically accurate. And if accurate, authoritative . . . which meant he had some apologizing to do. He needed to ask God for forgiveness and make things right with the Christ of the New Testament.

Seventeen

NICK

TWO HOURS LATER, Nick hit his knees on the floor of his dorm room. *God, I'm so sorry. I have been wrong about all this. I've been living in denial and running from You. Lord, I know that the Jesus in the Bible is Your Son. I believe He died to pay the penalty for my sin, and that He rose from the dead to prove He was sinless. Please forgive me for not believing. Forgive me for lusting, lying, and thinking only of myself. I want to live for You the rest of my life. Thanks for hearing me. Amen.*

In the weeks to come, Nick asked Jessica's forgiveness for sleeping with her—which seemed to surprise her—and he called his parents and former youth pastor to explain his turnaround. His youth pastor was thrilled and his mother cried on the phone, saying that her many prayers were being answered.

For the next several classes, Nick and the rest of the students seemed to enjoy Jamal's lectures. Nick felt he was not only growing intellectually, but also in his prayer life as he sought wisdom from God. The following Wednesday night, Nick got a call.

"Hey Nick."

"Jessica, how are you?"

"I'm doing great! You'll never believe this! I grabbed coffee with your friend Mina. Oh my, she is soooo sweet! We're getting into some great spiritual conversations. I'm really starting to get into all this stuff. When Mina talked about Jesus ticking off the religious leaders and reaching out to the poor and outcasts of society, I wish you could have heard her. She spoke about this time when Jesus talked to some woman who was getting water at a well. The woman was Samaritan, a race the Jewish people looked down on and didn't associate with. She had gone through a lot of relationships and was sort of an outcast, but Jesus seemed to really care about her and He gave her hope. I'm actually meeting with them again tomorrow morning at nine and I was wondering if you wanted to stop by."

"*Them?* Who else are you meeting with?"

"Oh, sorry. I asked Andrea to come too. Can you make it?"

"Sure, that'd be great. Where will you be?"

"Lower Greenville's Café Brazil."

What's this all about? Nick wondered. *Jessica taking initiative to talk about God?*

Nick was hopeful and skeptical at the same time. He still didn't completely trust her, yet he sensed a new enthusiasm in Jessica he had never seen. She'd already met with Mina, who didn't fit the picture of the superficial girls who normally surrounded Jessica. Not only that, but she had invited Andrea as well! Maybe God was doing something in her life.

Eighteen

THE EXTERNAL EVIDENCE TEST

NICK AND MINA sat at Café Brazil chatting about Jamal's class when Jessica and Andrea walked in together.

"What can I get you ladies?" asked the waitress.

"I'll just have a coffee," said Andrea.

"Me too," said Jessica.

"Very good. The coffee bar is self-serve, so help yourselves."

After several minutes of chatting, Nick pulled out his computer and began sharing with the girls what he learned.

"Before you guys showed up I was telling Mina that Jamal invited me to go with him yesterday and meet with a couple professors at Dallas Theological Seminary. Afterwards we drove over to Fort Worth and met with some professor at Southwestern who has a degree from Oxford. We talked about the friends and disciples of the apostle John who confirm the internal evidence that appears in the gospel accounts. I want to read a couple of things to you."

Nick found the page he wanted, then explained, "This is from a guy named Papias, who was bishop of Hierapolis during AD 130. The historian Eusebius preserves the writings of Papias as follows:

> The Elder (apostle John) used to say this also: "Mark, having been the interpreter of Peter, wrote down accurately all that he (Peter) mentioned. . . . For he was neither a hearer nor a companion of the Lord; but afterwards, as I said, he accompanied Peter, who adapted his teachings as necessity required, not as though he was making a compilation of the sayings of the Lord. So then Mark made no mistake writing down in this way some things as he mentioned them; for he paid attention to this one thing, not to omit anything that he had heard, not to include any false statement among them."[58]

"Ladies, this next reference is from Irenaeus," said Nick with a smile.

"Who was Irenaeus?" asked Jessica.

"He was a second-century church leader and a student of Polycarp, who was another close friend to the apostle John and the bishop of Smyrna. Irenaeus wrote about what he had learned from Polycarp:

Matthew published his gospel among the Hebrews (i.e. Jews) in their own tongue, when Peter and Paul were preaching the gospel in Rome and founding the church there. After their departure (i.e. death, which strong tradition places at the time of the Neronian persecution in AD 64), Mark, the disciple and interpreter of Peter himself handed down to us in writing the substance of Peter's preaching. Luke, the follower of Paul, set down in a book the gospel preached by his teacher. Then John, the disciple of the Lord, who also leaned on his breast (this is a reference to John 13:25 and 21:20) himself produced his Gospel, while he was living at Ephesus in Asia.[59]

"There's more, but I need a coffee refill. What's the best flavor?"

Andrea rolled her eyes. "Just hurry up. I have a question."

"Go ahead and sample them all, Nick. I'll try to answer this one," said Mina. "What's your question, Andrea?"

"If these guys were friends of John, weren't they biased?"

"That's a great question. When they wrote this, they

might have been somewhat biased. But, even if we didn't have the testimony of the early disciples and early church fathers, we would be able to conclude from such non-Christian writings as Josephus, the Talmud, Tacitus, and Pliny the Younger that, for one, Jesus did exist and was a Jewish teacher. We know that many people believed that He performed healings and exorcisms. Also, Jesus was rejected by the Jewish leaders. Non-Christian sources tell us He was crucified under Pontius Pilate in the reign of Tiberius. Critics admit that, despite His shameful death, His followers, who believed that He was still alive, spread beyond Palestine so that there were multitudes of them in Rome by AD 64. Lastly, all kinds of people from the cities and countryside—men and women, slave and free—worshiped Him as God by the beginning of the second century."[60]

Nineteen

DID THE DISCIPLES MAKE IT UP?

NICK SAT DOWN while Mina was rattling off facts from outside sources. "You know what I love about this place? There are so many flavors to choose from. So what did I miss?"

Jessica smiled. "Mina was telling Andrea that it is unlikely the early gospel writers were lying since non-Christian historians tell us the same things."

Nick responded immediately. "I used to think that because the disciples were biased they purposely mixed up the details. But I got to thinking about it. Why would they lie? Let's say they made up the resurrection. What was their motive? What did they get out of it? I'll tell you what they got out of it. Misunderstanding, rejection, persecution, torture, and martyrdom. Hardly a list of rewards!"[61]

"That's a really good point," said Jessica.

That's a really good point? She actually seems interested, Nick thought.

"The professor we met with from Dallas Theological Seminary gave me a quote from a book by Chuck Colson, who was a former aide to President Nixon. Colson went to prison over the Watergate scandal. Comparing his experience to that of the apostles, he writes:"

Watergate involved a conspiracy to cover up, perpetuated by the closest aides to the President of the United States . . . who were intensely loyal to their president. But one of them, John Dean . . . testified against Nixon, as he put it, "to save his own skin"—and he did so only two weeks after informing the president about what was really going on—two weeks! The real cover up, the lie, could only be held together for two weeks, and then everybody else jumped ship in order to save themselves. Now, the fact is that all that those around the president were facing was embarrassment, maybe prison. Nobody's life was at stake. But what about the disciples? Twelve powerless men, peasants really, were facing not just embarrassment or political disgrace, but beatings, stonings, and execution. Every single one of the disciples insisted, to their dying breaths, that they had seen Jesus bodily raised from the dead. Don't you think that one of those apostles would have cracked before being beheaded or stoned? . . . None did.[62]

"So all but one of them were killed for their faith?" asked Jessica.

"Not just killed for their faith. A lot of people die for their faith. These disciples died for what they saw with their own eyes."

"Maybe they were just really misled," commented Andrea.

"Are you kidding?" Nick shot back. "If they made up their claim of being eyewitnesses to a dead man coming back to life, they would have admitted it at the time. At least a few of them would have backed out to save their own lives. But that's not what happened. James was stoned to death. Peter was crucified on a cross. Paul was beheaded."

"Well, I'm just not buying it," said Andrea.

"Why not?" asked Nick.

"I'm just skeptical," said Andrea.

"Andrea, sometimes skepticism has its limitations," said Nick. "I mean, I'm glad you don't just want to have blind faith, but it's also possible to be too skeptical, you know? What if you were *always* skeptical about everything—like the GPS in your car, or what you're learning in all your other classes? Why be skeptical about what is *so* obvious? At some point, we all need to take steps of trust toward that which is reasonable."

Andrea crossed her arms as Nick continued, "Andrea, we've been friends for almost a year, and I like you a lot, so I'm going to shoot straight and tell you what I think. I think you are open to Jesus Christ. Otherwise you wouldn't be meeting with us and coming to Jamal's class. I can also tell you that the last several weeks of my life have been really different. I mean, I don't always feel spiritual and I still have questions and feelings of discouragement, but I think God revealed His Son to us in the New Testament. I don't know everything that means, but I know Christ died on the cross to pay the penalty for my sins and then He rose from the dead. Andrea, when I asked Him to forgive me for my sin, I *know* He did."

"You *have* been acting differently," said Andrea.

"I think so too," said Jessica. "You seem a lot happier. I think I want what you have."

Did she really just say that? Nick thought.

"Jessica, do you want Jesus Christ in your life?"

"I'm thinking about it."

Nick looked at Jessica and felt an adrenaline rush. "The decision to believe Jesus is God's Son and to ask Him to save you from your sin is not to be taken lightly. It might make you happier, but don't just do it for that reason. Do it because it's true. If you only want to feel good, it's easier to watch a movie or get a massage. There is a cost to following Jesus Christ as your guide and example. It's not a popular way to live. But if God is convicting you to believe, do it right away, even if you don't have one hundred percent of your questions answered."

"I will certainly think about it," said Jessica.

"I will too," said Andrea. "But I've still got my questions," she said, smiling.

The four talked more about Jesus, finished their coffee, and agreed to meet again.

Twenty

THE CANON

THE NEXT TIME Nick showed up for Jamal's class, he spotted Andrea in the back row and sat by her.

Jamal waded right in. "Today we'll be discussing the canon of Scripture. The word *canon* comes from the root word we translate *reed*. The English word is *cane* and the Greek is *kanon*. Years ago, the reed was used as a measuring rod, and came to mean 'standard.' The term *canon* was really coined by Origen, the third-century church father. Eventually the word came to mean 'list' or 'index.'[63] So this morning, when we refer to the canon, we are talking about an officially accepted list of books.[64]

"How many of you have read a Dan Brown novel like *The DaVinci Code* or *Lost Symbol*?" About a third of the class raised their hands.

"Yeah, those books are fun to read, but remember—they are *fiction*!" Jamal laughed. "Contrary to Brown, Constantine had nothing to do with creating the canon. I don't even believe the church *created* the canon. You guys look at me like I'm crazy. Honestly, I don't think the church *determined* which books would be called Scripture, the inspired Word of God. Rather, the church *recognized* or discovered which books had been inspired from their inception. Let me state that again. Class, I'd like you to write down my position regarding this issue. *A book is not the Word of God because it is accepted by the people of God. Rather, it is accepted by the people of God because it is the Word of God.* That is, God gives the book its divine authority. The people merely recognize the divine authority which God gives to it.[65]

"Now, many of my Catholic friends would believe that the church is the magistrate and regulator of the canon. Dr. Norman Geisler and William Nix note that the term 'apostolic' as used for the test of canonicity does not necessarily mean 'apostolic authorship,' or 'that which was prepared under the direction of the apostles.'[66] Luke, a close associate of Paul, was not an apostle, but Paul—who was an apostle—recognized Luke's work as authoritative. Okay,

I'm seeing a lot of blank looks. Are you tracking with me? Any questions?"

A guy Nick recognized from another class raised his hand. "Mr. Washington, I'm a little lost. I think I heard you say that the New Testament was approved by the apostles. What I want to know is what makes an apostle an apostle? I mean, lots of church signs and billboards mention apostles."

"Ha! Great question, Chad. And you're right about church signs—lots of people call themselves apostles these days. In fact, the folks at my uncle's church in Chicago call *him* 'Apostle Washington.' Now, I love my uncle, but I surely wouldn't put him in the same category as Peter and Paul. Some groups use the term loosely to describe leaders with larger-scope ministries—church planters, missionaries, and spiritual fathers. Whatever the case, the original apostles were in a class of their own. They were called and sent out by Jesus. They were 'the twelve.' Such apostles had to have been with Christ during His ministry and they had to be eyewitnesses of His resurrection. The apostle Paul was a unique case because he had an experience with Christ later on. However, when writing his first letter to the church at Corinth, he gave his apologia, or defense, for being an apostle. He said, 'Am I not an apostle? Have I not seen Jesus our Lord?'[67] In other words, his experience of seeing the resurrected Christ and being called out by Christ to share the gospel authenticated his apostleship."

Jamal walked across the front of the room. "The apostles had a role to 'speak for God.' The books in the New Testament were received and recognized by these apostles, and most of them were authored by an apostle. Does that help clarify who the apostles were?"

"Yes. Thank you."

"Anybody else have a question? Go ahead, Rodriguez."

"I know you mentioned Christ's words in the gospel of John, but what indication do we have that these apostles thought they were speaking for God?"

"Give me a second and I'll pull up the list for everybody to see."

Nick glanced at Andrea and saw she was taking notes.

After pulling up a new PowerPoint slide, Jamal continued, "This list is adapted from scholars Geisler and Turek. Here we go:

> - John recorded that the early believers believed that the apostles "are from God" (1 John 4:6).
> - John begins the book of Revelation with "The revelation of Jesus Christ, *which* God *gave him*" (Rev. 1:1).

Jamal pulled up the next slide.

> - Paul claimed that his letters were *"taught by the Spirit"* (1 Corinthians 2:13).
> - Paul claimed his writings are "the Lord's command" (1 Corinthians 14:37).
> - In Paul's first letter to the Thessalonians, Paul described his words *"as it actually is, the word of God"* (1 Thess. 2:13).
> - Paul quoted the gospels of Matthew and Luke, calling them "Scripture."

Jamal's next slide featured an early portrait of the apostle Peter.

> - Peter referred to Paul's letters (there are thirteen of them) and agreed they were inspired; he compares them to "the other Scriptures" (2 Pet. 3:15–16; see 2 Tim. 3:16).[68]

"Class, I'm going to put all these notes on Blackboard so you can check them out later. Any other questions?"

"I have a question based on our previous conversations," said Andrea. "If the apostles and the people of God were accepting these books very early on, why did it take so long to have them compiled in one volume?"

"Andrea, I don't know all the answers to that question, but I can share some reasonable speculation. For background, class, it wasn't until the Council of Hippo in AD 391 that the unified church recognized the canon as we now have it in our Bibles. Andrea, there was one practical reason the New Testament canon took almost three centuries to come into its present state. We know scrolls were very large—unlike today's books. It was harder to keep all the volumes in one place. Some of the most literate people in a community might only have a few scrolls. What a contrast to today where I can carry over a thousand books on my Kindle. Likewise, in that culture early Christians might never have dreamed of owning personal copies of all twenty-seven books of the New Testament.

"A second reason may have been persecution. You see, until AD 313, Christianity was pretty much illegal in the Roman Empire. The early Christians were often fleeing persecution. They couldn't just host a conference at the local university and openly discuss the canon. Much of the discussion was done in private, and they had to carefully hide and protect their scrolls. We do have indications that most of the books in our current New Testament were accepted as inspired and authoritative by Christians in the early centuries. From the beginning, Christians seemed to accept the four gospels, Acts, and Paul's letters. We have discovered *The Fragment of Muratori*, from the mid-second century, which included twenty-three of the New Testament books, and Iranaeus, writing in the early second century, quotes from twenty-four of the twenty-seven books. In the first three centuries, a few theologians had some questions about some of the shorter books—like Jude and 2 and 3 John. However, when the topic was finally brought to the table by church leaders in the fourth century, the inspired books seemed apparent to all. As Geisler explains, 'When the evidence was all on the table, all twenty-seven New Testament books, and only those twenty-seven books, were recognized as authentic.'"[69]

After lecturing awhile longer on the canon, Jamal wrapped up by discussing the requirements for the final papers. Nick walked out with Andrea.

"So, what do you think, Andrea?"

"I think I need a drink."

"Let's go to Café Brazil and talk about it."

"No, that's not what I meant, Nick. Jamal is making some good points about the Bible and I really don't want to think about this right now. I mean, if this stuff is all true, it could mean radical changes for me!"

Rather than press the issue, Nick decided to pray for her and let the Holy Spirit do His work.

Twenty-One

A MEMORIAL SERVICE IN PORTLAND

THE PRESBYTERIAN minister officiating at the packed memorial service in Portland focused on the family in the first row and said, "Barbara Peterson loved every one of you. She loved her sister Ruth and she loved her brother William. Bill, she told me about the times you all used to ride bikes, and of the April Fools' jokes she played on you when you were kids. Bill and Ruth, she wanted me to tell you that she prayed for you daily."

Lifting his eyes to the rest of the congregation, he said, "Barbara never married nor had physical children of her own, but oh, did she have spiritual children. The very fact that this sanctuary is overflowing with hundreds of people, and with so many standing in the back, testifies that she invested in lives. She used to say, 'My life is not my own. I belong to Jesus.' For the past six years, she spent two months every summer in Nigeria, serving orphanages. The hearts that have been touched through her life are now closer to God because of her faith. Before she died, I asked her what she would like me to say at her funeral. She said, 'Preach about Jesus and the hope that we have through His resurrection.' So I'd like to read about that hope in St. Paul's first letter to the Corinthians."

> For this corruptible must put on incorruption, and this mortal must put on immortality.
>
> So when this corruptible shall have put on incorruption, and this mortal shall have put on immortality, then shall be brought to pass the saying that is written, Death is swallowed up in victory.
>
> O death, where is thy sting? O grave, where is thy victory? The sting of death is sin; and the strength of sin is the law. But thanks be to God, which giveth us the victory through our Lord Jesus Christ.[70]

After Dr. William Peterson wiped the tears from his eyes with his handkerchief, he turned and glanced out across the auditorium. As his eyes drifted over the sea of faces, they came to rest on the large group standing near the back. *My goodness, look at all these people. Where did they all . . . wait a minute . . . no, that can't be!* But as he narrowed his gaze he began to nod. *Well I'll be. He flew in from Texas.*

An hour later, Nick greeted Dr. Peterson at the gravesite after some of the crowd had gone.

"Dr. Peterson, I'm very sorry for your loss."

"Nick, you didn't have to fly all the way out here to tell me that. You have school."

"Yes, but as a professor, you have meant so much to me. You and Mrs. Peterson had Jessica and me over several times last semester and I just felt I had to do something. I know you and your sister were close."

"Well, she was special and I'm sure she's in a better place."

Nick's face registered his surprise. "Do you mean heaven, Dr. Peterson? I thought you believed that heaven was more a state of mind than an actual place."

"Well, I'm not exactly sure, Nick. But my sister was a saint if there ever was one. And in times like this, I want to believe that heaven is true. I just don't know."

With a tear in his eye, the professor winked, as if optimistic about the thought of heaven.

Nick didn't really know what to say because it was a funeral and his instructor was grieving. Still, he was so surprised by Dr. Peterson's comment he blurted out, "You *can* know it's true! In the last month I've discovered that the Bible *is* true. I'm following Christ now and I am convinced that heaven is real."

Dr. Peterson rolled his eyes and placed his hand on Nick's shoulder. "Ah, Nick. I can see you've been spending time with my teaching assistant, Jamal. I love and respect Jamal, but let's talk about theology when I come back to town."

"Sorry, Dr. Peterson. I probably shouldn't have brought it up."

"No, it's good. I'm thinking through some things myself. I appreciate you, Nick. It's so kind of you to be here. In fact, you are by far the kindest student I've ever had."

Twenty-Two

RETHINKING TRUTH

ALTHOUGH the Petersons returned to Dallas two weeks later, Dr. Peterson decided to stay on leave for the rest of the semester. One evening, Dr. Peterson and his wife, Susan, invited Nick and Jessica over. Nick had told Dr. Peterson that he and Jessica were no longer dating, but that he felt comfortable bringing her since she seemed to connect well with Susan. During dinner the conversation shifted to Dr. Peterson's sister, Barbara.

"I've never known a woman who really lived her faith like Bill's sister," said Susan. "She was so dedicated to those orphans in Africa."

"She definitely had a heart of gold,"

said Dr. Peterson as he took a bite of grilled chicken.

"And convictions. Nick and Jessica—you should have heard her talk to her brother. She loved him so much she made a point to share her mind with him at every opportunity," said Susan.

"What do you mean?" asked Nick with a smile.

"Well, let's just say they had some lively debates on the matter of faith. She was a lot of fun even when we strongly disagreed. I'm going to miss her!" responded Susan.

"You know, she was probably more right than I gave her credit for," Dr. Peterson continued. "Looking back, I wish I would have been a bit more gracious to her, especially when we started talking about the other gospels."

"Why do say that?" asked Jessica.

"Well, I never really believed they were more reliable than the four gospels. I just wanted to prove to my sister that I was smarter than her and didn't want to agree with her limited views."

Nick set his fork down. "I thought at the beginning of class you said the other gospels were more reliable than the gospels in the New Testament."

"Nick, I've been fascinated about them for a long time, but I never did publish extensively on them because I knew they were filled with second- and third-century Gnosticism. During my sabbatical I've been reconsidering their truthfulness. If I am going to be honest, and if the New

Testament gospels are indeed trustworthy accounts, then there are considerable implications concerning the afterlife."

"I've heard that some of the faculty were in disagreement with Jamal teaching the New Testament as historically true," said Nick. "So you were never fully opposed to Jamal's teaching?"

"I knew what I was getting myself into when I offered Jamal the job. To be honest, though, my sister's death has me reconsidering the way I think about the Scriptures. The Gnostic gospels should be looked at and studied, but in no way do they undermine the four biblical gospels."

"Why not?" asked Jessica.

"Well, let's all go to my library and I'll let you take a look at some of them."

Twenty-Three

WHAT ABOUT
THE OTHER
GOSPELS?

AFTER DINNER, Dr. Peterson took Nick and Jessica into his library.

"Wow, your library is huge!" exclaimed Nick as he stared at the impressive shelves of scholarly volumes.

"Over here I have some copies of the Gnostic gospels," said Dr. Peterson. "Some of these like *Truth, Thomas, Philip, Egyptians,* and *Mary* were included in the Nag Hammadi Library, published in English in 1977."

"What exactly is Gnosticism?" asked Jessica.

"Gnosticism was a school of thought —actually more than one school of thought—that sought salvation through secret knowledge. Perhaps two of the more popular Gnostic works are the *Gospel of Thomas* and the *Infancy Gospel of Thomas*. Here is the collection. Take a look at it,"[71] responded Dr. Peterson.

He took the small book and handed it to Jessica.

She flipped through a few pages.

Dr. Peterson grinned. "Go ahead and read some of it out loud to Nick."

"Jesus said, 'Blessed is the lion which the man shall eat, and the lion become man; and cursed is the man whom the lion shall eat, and the lion become man.'"[72]

"What is that all about? It makes no sense," commented Nick.

"Funny you should say that, Nick. I actually agree, but a few years ago I received an elite invitation and honorarium to teach on the subject with a scholar from Princeton. It was odd because quite a few feminist theologians in the audience were into this theory that the Gnostic gospels had a higher view of women than the ordinary gospels. I agreed with them at the time, but it didn't set well in my mind. Let me show you something. Jessica, turn to end of the *Gospel of Thomas*—right here—and read."

Jessica took it and read aloud, "Simon Peter said to them, 'Let Mary go forth from among us, for women are not worthy of the life.' Jesus said: 'Behold, I shall lead her, that I may make her male, in order that she also may become a living spirit like you males. For every woman who makes herself male shall enter the kingdom of heaven.'"[73]

Jessica stopped reading. "Um, I see what you mean. I guess I would have to become a male to enter heaven!"

"When were these other gospels written?" asked Nick.

"Good question, Nick. No one believes that the apostle Thomas was the real author of the *Gospel of Thomas*. Scholars generally consider it to have been written well into the second century and the *Infancy Gospel of Thomas* no earlier. Similarly, the *Gospel of Philip* and the *Gospel of Mary* can be dated no earlier than the second century, perhaps into the third century."[74]

"You mean, like, a hundred years after Jesus' lifetime?" asked Jessica.

"At least." Dr. Peterson nodded.

At that point Susan Peterson came in and announced dessert. "Who would like some cherry pie and coffee?"

"Sounds great," said Nick.

Twenty-Four

THE TRUE GOSPEL

"THIS IS DELICIOUS," said Jessica around a mouthful of pie.

Nick finished his completely before speaking. "Okay, Dr. Peterson, I don't fully understand. When I first took your class back in the fall, your teachings—along with some of the books you recommended by scholars like Bart Ehrman—encouraged me to question my trust in the Bible. But after investigating the matter with Jamal these past couple of months and talking to other professors at Dallas Seminary, Redeemer, and Southwestern, I've become convinced that the New Testament is historically reliable. And since it *is* historically trustworthy, I found it necessary to reconsider the person of Jesus Christ, His work on the cross, and His resurrection. Do you believe that Jesus Christ is God's Son who died for your sins and rose again?"

"I'm not sure," said Dr. Peterson.

"All you have to do is believe in Him. Salvation is not by our works, but by God's grace, through trusting in Christ's deity, death, and resurrection. Do you believe that?"

"Well—it's not that simple, Nick."

"Yes it is!" Nick shot back. "You mentioned that your sister is in heaven. Why do you believe in heaven? What's your basis?"

Nick paused, suddenly realizing how bold he was getting with his professor.

"Well, Susan has a more positive attitude toward Scripture and the church than I have, but I'm still wrestling with some questions intellectually. You must realize I have never expressed all my perplexities in the classroom."

"What's a specific question that's troubling you?" asked Nick, hoping Dr. Peterson wouldn't ask a complicated question he couldn't answer.

"Well, I still wrestle with the variants in the copies we have."

"I did too, Professor, but do you know Dr. Daniel Wallace? As a professor, he concluded that we *can* be confident with what the original books in the Bible said."

"Well, of course I know Dan, and I've read all of his books. Nick, I've always respected your boldness and searching heart. You remind me a lot of myself when I was your age."

"Well, are you willing to repent of your sin and trust what Christ did for you on the cross?" asked Nick.

Dr. Peterson laughed louder. "You like to get right to the point, don't you? You're like a young Billy Graham."

"You know, Bill, I think Nick has a good point," Susan said. "I've been wanting to get back to reading the Bible. As a child I remember talking to Jesus frequently. I feel like I miss Him. Maybe we should consider getting reconnected with the church."

Nick did not want the conversation detoured. "Church involvement is important, Mrs. Peterson, but remember that salvation is by God's grace. A verse I recently memorized in Romans says, 'Now when a man works, his wages are not credited to him as a gift, but as an obligation. However, to the man who does not work but trusts God who justifies the wicked, his faith is credited as righteousness.'[75] Dr. Peterson, I know you have read church history more than me and can read Romans in the Greek, but I was wondering if you have ever specifically trusted Christ's atoning death for your sins?"

"Nick, come on. Do you think you can convince me of something I've spent my entire career studying?"

"Well, I'm not sure. But if God's Spirit is convicting you, don't resist Him."

"It's just a lot to swallow and such a narrow interpretation," sighed Dr. Peterson.

"Bill, be nice," said Susan.

Dr. Peterson continued, "Nick knows I love and respect him. Tell you what. You all know that I have been rethinking some things, but I'm not about to start faking some personal relationship like Christians talk about. Academically, I believe the historical Christ is perhaps different than the one Christians see in the New Testament."

"But you know the New Testament was written by eyewitnesses and those who interviewed eyewitnesses, right, Dr. Peterson?"

"Nick, let's talk about it later."

Nick wanted to press him further, but he could tell Dr. Peterson was not about to be pushed into anything he could not academically accept.

"All right," said Nick, smiling. "Later."

Dr. Peterson changed the topic to the Dallas Mavericks' NBA playoff run, and after a little while, Nick and Jessica left. They had not talked much with each other, and he felt kind of awkward for even bringing her along. Nick also felt bad for raising his voice to Dr. Peterson. He hoped his aggressive questioning had not turned the professor off. Did his preaching make any difference to a scholar? He thought of several statements he now wished he could go back and say differently. In fact, he began to feel sick about it—like he had blown a good opportunity and maybe said too much. Maybe he should call Jamal, but he did not want to disclose any of the personal—and confidential—conversation he just had with Dr. Peterson. Peterson had probably shared more honestly with him than he ever had with any other student. Nick was still in a daze of discouragement as he dropped Jessica off at her apartment.

Little did he know that, thirty minutes later, Jessica would be calling Mina.

"I need to talk to you about God."

"Sure," said Mina.

"Look, I don't want Nick to think I'm just doing this for him, so that's why I'm calling you. I want to start believing in Christ like you do."

"Jessica, if your heart is ready, it's pretty simple. In your own words, tell God that you've sinned against Him. For example, when I first came to God I told Him that I was a self-centered, prideful gossiper who put other gods—like boys and material possessions—above Him."

"Mina, I can't imagine you being like that at all."

"Oh, I was far worse than you will ever know! But by God's grace I have been set free. Romans 3:23 says, 'For all have sinned and fall short of the glory of God.' That includes you and me. A few chapters later it says, 'The wages of sin is death.' Sin is serious and our first step in coming to God is to get real, admit our transgressions, and ask for His forgiveness."

"You're right. I've really lived for myself and been a jerk to a lot of people."

"Jessica, the good news is that in spite of your sin—your very worst sin—God loves you. Scripture tells us in Romans 5:8, 'But God demonstrates his own love for us in this: While we were still sinners, Christ died for us.' Christ died for you, Jessica. That's why that famous verse John 3:16 says, 'For God so loved the world that he gave his one and only Son, that whoever believes in him shall not perish but have eternal life.'"

"I love that verse."

"Well, if you want, you can pray right now on the phone. Would you like to?"

"Yes." Jessica felt her heart beating fast and hands getting sweaty. She knew she was about to make the most significant decision of her life. A sudden hesitation filled her mind as she wondered what words she would use in talking to Almighty God. Mina seemed to read her mind and alleviated this concern before Jessica could express it.

"Jessica, when we pray to God, our prayer does not have to be perfect. Remember you are talking to a loving Father who invites us to come to Him. Just speak from your heart, confess your sin, and acknowledge you are trusting

Christ's work on the cross for your salvation."

"Okay, I'll do it now." After a pause, Jessica began in a sincere voice, "Well, God, I want to tell You that I need You in my life. Mina is right, I am a sinner. I know I've failed You and turned away from You many, many times. I've lied and gossiped, I've been wasted many times, and I've slept with several boyfriends. I even made fun of Nick and others who had faith in You. God, I now believe Your Word is true. So I believe Jesus is Your Son and I want Him to be the Savior and Lord of my life. Thank You, Jesus, for dying to pay the penalty for my sin. Please have mercy on me like that woman at the well Mina told me about several weeks ago. Thank You, God. Amen."

Mina rushed over to Jessica's apartment and the two friends hugged and laughed and talked past two in the morning. This night would be better than any party or celebration Jessica had ever attended. She now had a wonderful sense of peace that had evaded her all her life. It seemed like she was beginning an exciting new chapter in a long book that previously contained lots of heartache, sadness, and confusion. This night, however, was a new beginning and a time for great joy and celebration on earth as well as in the cosmos, for the Bible says, "There is rejoicing in the presence of the angels of God over one sinner who repents."[76]

The Coffeehouse Chronicles series includes:

Is the Bible True . . . Really?
Who Is Jesus . . . Really?
Did the Resurrection Happen . . . Really?

NOTES

1. See Bart Ehrman, *Misquoting Jesus: The Story Behind Who Changed the Bible and Why* (New York: Harper Collins, 2005), 7.

2. See Ehrman, *Misquoting Jesus*, 89.

3. Ibid., 24.

4. Gregory A. Boyd and Paul Rhodes Eddy, *Lord or Legend?: Wrestling with the Jesus Dilemma* (Grand Rapids: Baker, 2007), 52–53.

5. See Ehrman, *Misquoting Jesus*, 89.

6. 1 John 1:9

7. J. Z. Smith. "Dying and Rising Gods," in *Encyclopedia of Religion*, ed. M. Eliade, vol. 4 (New York: Macmillan, 1987), 521. Quoted by Boyd and Eddy, *Lord or Legend?*, 53.

8. Boyd and Eddy, *Lord or Legend?*, 53.

9. "Did Christ Rise from the Dead?," from Lee Strobel's website. Accessed August 28, 2010, http://www.leestrobel.com/videoserver/video.php?clip=strobelT1115.

10. See Josh McDowell, *The DaVinci Code: A Quest for Answers* (Holiday, FL: Green Key Books, 2006), 38.

11. Richard Gordon, *Image and Value in the Graeco-Roman World* (Aldershot, UK: Variorum, 1996), 96. Quoted by McDowell, *The DaVinci Code*, 38.

12. Bruce M. Metzger, "Mystery Religions and Early Christianity," in *Historical and Literary Studies* (Leiden, Netherlands: E. J. Brill, 1968), 11. Quoted by McDowell, *The DaVinci Code*, 38.

13. Edwin M. Yamauchi, *Pre-Christian Gnosticism*, 2nd ed. (Grand Rapids: Baker Book House, 1983), 112. Quoted by McDowell, *The DaVinci Code*, 38.

14. M. J. Vermaseren, *Mithras: The Secret God* (London: Chatto and Windus, 1963). Quoted by McDowell, *The DaVinci Code*, 38.

15. John F. Walvoord and Roy B. Zuck, eds., *The Bible Knowledge Commentary: Old Testament* (Wheaton: Victor Books, 1985), 1573.

16. Norman L. Geisler and William E. Nix, *A General Introduction to the Bible* (Chicago: Moody Press, 1968), 24; David Ewert, *A General Introduction to the Bible: From Ancient Tablets to Modern Translations* (Grand Rapids: Zondervan, 1983), 104–108; and E. Wurthwein, *The Text of the Old Testament: An Introduction to the Biblia Hebraica*, trans., Errol F. Rhodes (Grand Rapids: Eerdmans, 1979), 49–53.

17. McDowell, *The DaVinci Code*, 15.

18. Mark 2:23–28

19. See Ehrman, *Misquoting Jesus*, 9.

20. Ibid.

21. Lee Strobel, *The Case for the Real Jesus* (Grand Rapids: Zondervan, 2007), 74.

22. Boyd and Eddy, *Lord or Legend?*, 22–23.

23. Ibid., 23.

24. Millar Burrows, *What Mean These Stones? The Significance of Archeology for Biblical Studies* (New York: Meridian Books, 1956), 52. Quoted by Josh McDowell and Sean McDowell, *More Than a Carpenter* (Carol Stream, IL: Tyndale, 2009), 64.

25. William F. Albright, *Recent Discoveries in Bible Lands* (New York: Funk and Wagnalls, 1955), 136. Quoted by McDowell and McDowell, *More Than a Carpenter*, 65.

26. McDowell and McDowell, *More Than a Carpenter*, 65–66.

27. Sir William Ramsay, *The Bearing of Recent Discovery on the Trustworthiness of the New Testament* (London: Hodder and Stoughton, 1915), 222. Quoted by McDowell and McDowell, *More Than a Carpenter*, 65–66.

28. Colin J. Hemer, *The Book of Acts in the Setting of Hellenistic History* (Winona Lake, Ind.: Eisenbrauns, 1990). Quoted by Norman L. Geisler and Frank Turek, *I Don't Have Enough Faith to Be an Atheist* (Wheaton: Crossway Books, 2004), 256–62.

29. Acts 17:6

30. F. F. Bruce, "Archaeological Confirmation of the New Testament," in *Revelation and the Bible*, ed. Carl Henry (Grand Rapids: Baker Book House, 1969), 325.

31. Edward Musgrave Blaiklock, *Layman's Answer: An Examination of the New Theology* (London: Hodder and Stoughton, 1968), 36.

32. Brian L. Janeway, "The Acts of the Apostles and the Archaeologists," in *Bible and Spade 12:2* (Spring 1999), 56.

33. F. F. Bruce, "Archaeological Confirmation of the New Testament," in *Revelation and the Bible*, ed. Carl Henry, 321.

34. McDowell and McDowell, *More Than a Carpenter*, 70–71.

35. See McDowell and McDowell, *More Than a Carpenter*, 71.

36. F. F. Bruce, *The New Testament Documents: Are They Reliable?* (Downers Grove, IL: InterVarsity, 1964), 16. Quoted by McDowell and McDowell, *More Than a Carpenter*, 71.

37. McDowell and McDowell, *More Than a Carpenter*, 71–72.

38. Bruce Metzger, quoted in Lee Strobel, *The Case for Christ* (Grand Rapids: Zondervan, 1998), 60. Quoted by McDowell and McDowell, *More Than a Carpenter*, 72.

39. Ibid.

40. Personal correspondence from Dan Wallace, January 6, 2003. Quoted by McDowell and McDowell, *More Than a Carpenter*, 73.

41. Strobel, *The Case for the Real Jesus*, 70.

42. Craig L. Blomberg, "The Historical Reliability of the New Testament," in William Lane Craig, *Reasonable Faith* (Wheaton: Crossway, 1994), 226. Quoted by McDowell and McDowell, *More Than a Carpenter*, 75.

43. McDowell and McDowell, *More Than a Carpenter*, 76.

44. J. Ed Komoszewski, M. James Sawyer, Daniel B. Wallace, *Reinventing Jesus* (Grand Rapids: Kregel, 2006), 215. Quoted by McDowell and McDowell, *More Than a Carpenter*, 76.

45. McDowell and McDowell, *More Than a Carpenter*, 76.

46. Geisler and Turek, *I Don't Have Enough Faith to Be an Atheist*, 228.

47. Komoszewski, Sawyer, and Wallace, *Reinventing Jesus*, 215. Quoted by McDowell and McDowell, *More Than a Carpenter*, 77.

48. McDowell and McDowell, *More Than a Carpenter*, 77.

49. John Warwick Montgomery, *Where Is History Going?* (Grand Rapids: Zondervan, 1969), 46. Quoted by McDowell and McDowell, *More Than a Carpenter*, 77.

50. John McRay, quoted in Lee Strobel, *The Case for Christ*, 97.

51. 2 Peter 1:16–17 NLT

52. John 19:35 NLT

53. McDowell and McDowell, *More Than a Carpenter*, 80–81.

54. Acts 2:22 NASB

55. Acts 26:24–26 NLT

56. McDowell and McDowell, *More Than a Carpenter*, 81.

57. F. F. Bruce, *The New Testament Documents: Are they Reliable?*, 33. Quoted by McDowell and McDowell, *More Than a Carpenter*, 80–81.

58. Eusebius, *Ecclesiastical History*, bk. 3, chap. 39. Quoted by McDowell and McDowell, *More Than a Carpenter*, 84–85.

59. Irenaeus, *Against Heresies*, 3.1.1. Quoted by McDowell and McDowell, *More Than a Carpenter*, 85–86.

60. Michael J. Wilkins and J. P. Moreland, eds. *Jesus Under Fire: Modern Scholarship Reinvents the Historical Jesus* (Grand Rapids: Zondervan, 1995), 222.

61. Adapted from Peter Kreeft, quoted in Geisler and Turek, *I Don't Have Enough Faith to Be an Atheist.*

62. Chuck Colson, quoted in Geisler and Turek, *I Don't Have Enough Faith to Be an Atheist*, 292–93.

63. F. F. Bruce, *The Books and the Parchments: How We Got Our English Bible* (Old Tappan, NJ: Fleming H. Revell, 1950), 95. Quoted by Josh McDowell, *The New Evidence That Demands a Verdict* (Nashville: Thomas Nelson Publishers, 1999), 21.

64. Ralph Earle, *How We Got Our Bible* (Grand Rapids: Baker Book House, 1971), 31. Quoted by McDowell, *The New Evidence That Demands a Verdict*, 21.

65. Geisler and Nix, *A General Introduction to the Bible*, 221. Quoted by McDowell, *The New Evidence That Demands a Verdict*, 22.

66. Ibid.

67. 1 Corinthians 9:1

68. Geisler and Turek, *I Don't Have Enough Faith to Be an Atheist*, 364–65.

69. Ibid., 370.

70. 1 Corinthians 15:53–57 KJV

71. McDowell, *The DaVinci Code*, 21.

72. "Infancy Gospel of Thomas," in *The Lost Books of the Bible and the Forgotten Books of Eden* (Dallas: Word Publishing, 1994), 7. Quoted by McDowell, *The DaVinci Code*, 21.

73. "The Gospel of Thomas," 114. Quoted by McDowell, *The DaVinci Code*, 22.

74. *The Lost Books of the Bible and the Forgotten Books of Eden*, 246–47. Quoted by McDowell, *The DaVinci Code*, 23.

75. Romans 4:4–5

76. Luke 15:10

ACKNOWLEDGMENTS

WE WOULD LIKE to thank Randall Payleitner, our acquisitions editor at Moody Publishers, for his extensive work and outstanding services to help make this book possible. Also, we thank Paul Santhouse for his excellent editing, and Clay Sterrett (Dave's father) and Melissa Kibby for reading the initial manuscript and providing feedback, corrections, and encouragement.

The authors are grateful for permission to use the following copyrighted material:

Excerpts from *More Than a Carpenter*, by Josh McDowell and Sean McDowell, © 2009 by Josh McDowell and Sean McDowell. Used by permission of Tyndale House Publishers.

Excerpts from *The New Evidence That Demands a Verdict*, by Josh McDowell, ©1999 by Josh McDowell. Used by permission of Thomas Nelson Publishers.

The Coffee House Chronicles

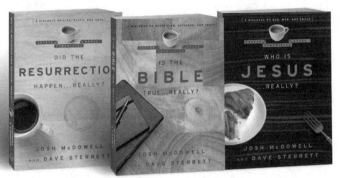

ISBN-13: 978-0-8024-8768-1

ISBN-13: 978-0-8024-8766-7

ISBN-13: 978-0-8024-8767-4

With over 40 million books sold, bestselling author Josh McDowell is no stranger to creatively presenting biblical truth. Now, partnering with fellow apologist Dave Sterrett, Josh introduces a new series targeted at the intersection of story and truth.

The Coffee House Chronicles are short, easily devoured novellas aimed at answering prevalent spiritual questions. Each book in the series tackles a long-contested question of the faith, and then answers these questions with truth through relationships and dialogue in each story.

MOODY PUBLISHERS

www.MoodyPublishers.com

Why Trust Jesus?

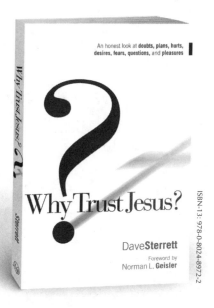

Our generation is up for grabs! Our trust has been shattered in other areas as we have seen hypocrisy in governmental leaders as well as in the church. We are looking for relationships that are authentic and full of life, but we have many questions in regard to faith, reason, suffering and even the person of Jesus himself.

MOODY
PUBLISHERS

www.MoodyPublishers.com

Just Do Something

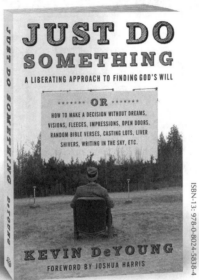

Hyperspiritual approaches to finding God's will just don't work. It's time to try something new: give up. God doesn't need to tell us what to do at each fork in the road. He's already revealed His plan for our lives: to love Him with our whole hearts, to obey His Word, and after that, to do what we like. No need for hocus-pocus. No reason to be directionally challenged. *Just Do Something.*

MOODY
PUBLISHERS

www.MoodyPublishers.com

READ THE STORY.

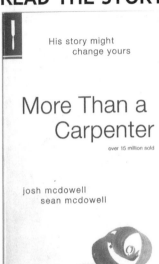

His story might change yours

More Than a Carpenter

over 15 million sold

josh mcdowell
sean mcdowell

Available in 6-pack or 30-pack sets for best value.

Since its original publication in 1977, this modern classic has over 15 million copies in print and has introduced countless people to Jesus. Now, in this newly updated version, Josh and his son Sean reexamine the evidence for today's generation: Is Jesus really the Lord he claimed to be?

WEIGH THE FACTS.

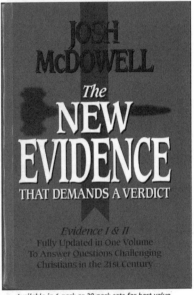

Maintaining its classic defense of the faith, this fully updated volume provides a wealth of historical, archaeological, and bibliographical evidences for the basic tenets of Christian belief.

Available in 6-pack or 30-pack sets for best value.

ORDER YOURS TODAY!
Visit www.josh.org/store or your favorite bookseller.